10 June 18

The Emotionally Secure Couple:

The Key to Everything You Want in a Healthy Relationship

By Joe Martino

For Erica.
Without her, nothing I've done would have been
possible.
Erica, I love you.
To my children, I hope that you will always chase
courageously after healthy relationships.

Table of Contents

Foreword

WHEN I READ *THE EMOTIONALLY SECURE COUPLE*, I hear Joe's voice. I love hearing the author's voice when I'm reading the words they've chosen to describe their thoughts and feelings.

But I think what I love most about this book is that I can hear Joe's *heart*.

I've known Joe ever since we were classmates in college and I've watched him transform as his pastor before my very eyes . He has come from abject brokenness in his past and unlike so many, he has faced his hurt and decided to heal. You have to decide to heal—it doesn't just happen, nor can someone make it happen for you. How Joe would choose to describe it would be "taking ownership" of your life. No blaming, no framing, no shaming in order to deflect personal responsibility. Joe doesn't just write about this clinically or academically; he has walked out these words he

1

shares with you and miraculously lived to tell about it. Those are my favorite books to read.

Of all the things that Joe does as a counselor, the thing he has leveraged his life for is marriages. He believes in marriage with every fiber of his being and feels a calling to specifically help marriages survive and thrive. He will walk into a burning house and fight to salvage every living thing possible in hope that he might save the marriage, and thus, the home. He bleeds for couples who are bleeding. He walks into the hard places with couples—the unspeakable places in their hearts—and seeks to show them *hope* when they are feeling a resounding *nope* in their spirit.

From the first paragraph of this book, it was clear to me that Joe isn't interested in writing to show you how special he is. He is writing to let people know how special they are and how delicate and complex and difficult and beautiful and terrifying and wonderful the gift of marriage is. He doesn't sugarcoat a single thing, nor does he mince words to soften the blow of truth as he writes. I never felt a judgmental, condescending spirit that only adds more weight to the existing burdens of life.

You may for the first time in your dating relationship or marriage feel normalized in your experiences of heartache and heartbreak, which will open new possibilities for reconciliation and redemption when you felt like a lost cause in a relationship that was game over in your mind with one or both parties resting their finger on the kill switch. Joe was made for this moment, and this book will show you his comfort in places that would make most people cave.

I will say it again: I know Joe and have witnessed how he has redeemed personal torture into emotion transformation. He had so many people give him a death wish for his relationship with his wife, Erica, even before their wedding day and I can say unreservedly that his marriage is one of the strongest I know of. This wasn't and isn't easy, but that's precisely why it sets itself apart, because he faces things head-on instead of living in denial, hoping something will happen to make it better. He owns his decisions and isn't afraid to make the hard changes to create a healthy marriage.

I've learned a great deal from Joe and I can't wait for you to see the things that God has walked him through and worked him through in order to share with such honesty and honor regarding the sacred covenant of marriage. These pages are teeming with stories of salvation and handholds of hope. I think you'll find yourself having a hard time putting it down.

~Jason Holdridge, Lead Pastor of Impact Church

Introduction:

Is Your Marriage Mortal?

THIS BOOK CAME FROM ONE SIMPLE QUESTION: Is my marriage mortal? The more I thought about it, the more I knew that indeed my marriage was mortal. In fact, every relationship I have is mortal. As surely as my body can wither and die, so can my relationships. So can yours. Part of the problem is that we fail to take ownership of this idea. We fail to admit that our relationship is a delicate, fragile creation that can die. I think deep down we know it can die, but we deny it, which creates a false sense of security for us. It allows us to believe that maybe if we deny it and pretend like it could never happen to us, it won't. This never works. Perhaps it is because we all have other friendships that died and we're not sure why they ceased. In an effort to avoid that pain, we pretend that our most important relationship cannot die.

You may recognize parts of your own story in the

stories I share. They are a collection of real people I have met over the years mixed into fictional characters to protect names and identities. We all know the statistics. Depending on what you read, out of one hundred couples getting married this weekend, a little over one-half of them will get divorced and relatively soon at that. Of course, if we lined up one hundred couples, I bet that almost every one of them would assume that it is the mythical "someone else" who will end up divorced. Certainly not them. They are in love. They are committed to working it out.

The numbers of infidelity are even more staggering. Some research suggests that 40 to 70 percent of partners cheat on their spouses. Of course, we all think that will happen to the "other guy." But the problem with that kind of thinking is to the other guy, *I am* the other guy. In other words, it could happen to all of us. Any one of us could end up being unfaithful or having a spouse who is unfaithful. Any one of us could end up divorced. The numbers do not lie. We need to accept that fact first and foremost.

When we do not take responsibility and ownership of this fact, we tend to blame the other person only.

It's my spouse's fault.
I'm this way because my dad wasn't the dad he should have been.
I'm this way because my mom was a controlling person.

We blame everyone and everything but our own actions.

One day, I was sitting in a coffee shop writing, and I couldn't help but hear the man sitting next to me talking about his marriage. To his credit, he obviously realized it was in trouble. To his detriment, he seemed to think it was only in trouble because of his wife's actions. He thought that once she changed, the relationship would work beautifully. Champagne would fall from the heavens, people would stand up and cheer, and so on. The truth was that his wife may have been at fault, but I guarantee you that if he would allow me to dig into his relationship, I would find that he is guilty of a few mistakes too. In fact, just sitting there listening to what he said convinced me of that truth. Besides, it's impossible for him to "fix" his wife. It is impossible for him to change his dad, mom, or whomever else he blames for his life. He can only take responsibility for himself. He can only change himself. He can only fix his mistakes and take responsibility for his part in the relationship.

This is not just true for him and married couples— it is true for everyone. We cannot experience the life we want to experience until we take ownership for our own actions. We must ask deep questions of ourselves. If I am unhappy in my relationship with my wife, I should ask myself some deeply hard and potentially disturbing questions about my own actions in the relationship. If I carry hurt from my childhood, I must be willing to explore them. I need to be willing to look at how they might be affecting my relationship with my wife, my kids, and those around me. I must ask myself if I have done everything I can to make the relationship right. This is not only hard, but it is also scary and aims right to the core of my pride.

Of course, there will be relationships that cannot be fixed. The other person will not engage; they will not allow their partner inside. In those rare cases, it is imperative that you and I can honestly say, "I tried everything." A marriage never *has* to end in divorce. No relationship has to end on bad terms. When they do, it is because someone refuses to move away from hurt toward the other person.

Your marriage can be everything you ever hoped and dreamed it could be. If you are both willing to take an honest look at your own actions, attitudes, and emotions and how they impact your relationship, you can have the relationship you want to have. You can have hope. You can have happiness. It will require you to give up your demand that your spouse change. It will probably require you to learn a new way to communicate. It will require you to engage in conflict with your partner and wade into emotional waters that feel unsafe, deep, dark, and scary.

The Emotionally Secure Couple will give you the skills to swim comfortably in those waters. It will require you to go to a few places in your heart that you may not want to go near. You may end up exploring some old hurts that you thought you had dealt with. It will probably be painful at some point, but I promise it will be worth it.

Chapter 1:

What If?

DEREK SAT ON THE COUCH IN MY OFFICE. HIS Adam's apple moved up and down in rhythm with his labored breathing. He was obviously distressed. The first few moments of the first session are like a dance: the two partners don't know how to act without any music to guide them. Therapist and client must listen for the music that is not there and end up in synchrony.

Derek looked at me and said, "My wife and I just can't get on the same page. Forget communication—we can't even agree on what we need to communicate!"

I said, "But what if I could teach you how to talk to her and how she could talk to you and move you through your conflict? What if you could engage conflict in a way that improved your relationship? What if you and your wife could actually repair your marriage?"

Derek and Ruby had been married for a few years

when they walked into my office. Things started to fall apart quickly. Derek moved out and into an apartment. Ruby begged him to come home. Derek stayed away. She begged some more.

Until she stopped.

After begging, she became incensed. First, she was hurt. Then she was angry. Rage and bitterness followed next. Finally, she flirted with contempt. Overarching these emotions was numbness.

She clung to numbness to protect her heart. At a different time, Ruby sat in my office and told me, "I'm not mad at Derek. I'm not. I'm not angry, I'm not sad; I'm not… anything. I'm just really tired."

If I were going to help them, I would have to challenge her numbness and teach them both a way to talk that moved their relationship forward. I worried that I would run out of time before I could help them.

And I almost did.

One day, Derek walked in and told me that Ruby had decided she was done. She wanted a divorce. "The worst part is that she thinks I was drunk, and I swear to you I wasn't. I hadn't even had three beers in two days!"

Derek was angry. I asked him how he responded to Ruby.

"Respond? I just kind of walked away."

"What if you could change that?" I asked.

What if, indeed!

About a week later, Derek and Ruby walked into my office and she told me, "I want to make our relationship work."

I asked why she had changed her mind. Derek responded for her.

Derek had gone over to her house and rather than shrinking in the face of her typical haze-and-raze approach to their conflict, he engaged her. He used the same principles that I've written in this book to begin the healing process of their relationship. He wasn't mean. He wasn't caustic. He was direct. He told her how he felt. He engaged his feelings while validating hers. He told her that he loved her, but he gave her the freedom to leave and walk away. For maybe the first time in their life as a married couple, he stopped trying to control her and gave their relationship the opportunity to grow or fail.

This is one of the keys to a healthy relationship: allowing it the opportunity to fail. We'll talk more about this later, but for Derek, it was revolutionary. It saved his marriage. And you'll need to embrace it to create the relationship you want.

I'll ask you the same question: What if you didn't have to go through Derek's situation? What if you could create habits in your life that would create a healthy relationship as a byproduct? What if you could learn new strategies to create a healthy marriage?

I believe you can do exactly that, and this book is my attempt to help you create those habits.

We will come back to Derek and Ruby later to see how they navigated these habits. By the way, as of the writing of this book, they are expecting their first baby.

ARE YOU CONTRIBUTING?

Eric and Emily had called my office and had asked to meet with me at a coffee shop. I agreed. Their relationship was in real trouble.

They knew it.

Sadly, no one else knew.

From the outside, they had done everything right. They had been friends before dating. They dated for almost a year before he proposed. A year later, they were married.

Twenty months later, they were sitting in that coffee shop with me surrounded by a throng of hipsters listening to indie music while wearing knit hats in the summer.

Both had great jobs. Both wanted their relationship to work—at least in the beginning.

Tears flowed down Emily's face as she told her side of the story. Eric sat with a face carved from granite as she talked about her infidelity. She cried. He withdrew. She stressed that no sexual activity happened— besides a few light kisses and the occasional hug. Her assurances did nothing to thaw Eric's face or emotions. "It just happened. I wasn't looking for it," she implored.

At that line, I saw my first glimpse of Eric's emotions. He was angry. Of course, that's understandable. What I was about to ask him, though, would start a fire in our conversation.

"Eric, what do you think you did to contribute to this situation?"

Raw, white anger boiled across his face.

"Me?!"

"He was just never home. He just wasn't… there." Emily slowly and deliberately pushed the words out for me. Eric's response told me that this was not the first time they had had this conversation. His shoulders rolled and his head shook, his face screaming contempt without a word escaping his mouth.

Both had come from homes where their parents and grandparents had divorced and remarried, with one parent on both sides being remarried multiple times. Emily was the result of her mom's first affair.

She was horrified at the prospect of having become a cheater. Despite whatever reasons she had to justify her actions, she felt as though she had become the very thing she always wanted to avoid.

Eric's father was a good provider but was never present emotionally.

Perhaps this was the hardest pill for them to swallow: they had become the parent they most struggled with in their own childhood. This is, of course, very common. Children learn what they live, and live what they learn.

As with most things in couples counseling, this principle seems to be so plain, so obvious that it almost seems not to warrant utterance.

And yet, often the most basic things are the ones we

overlook the most. Our parents, or primary caregivers as children, blueprint us for how we will interact emotionally as adults. They give us the plan that we utilize, often without us realizing that we are repeating what they do.

We often default to the patterns of living we learned in childhood. This is true even if we have intellectually rejected them. Rejecting them without replacing them only creates a vacuum that we often don't know how to fill, so we return to what we know.

Eric and Emily had been taught how to save money, take care of a home, and provide all of life's basic necessities. They had never been taught how to answer the core questions that haunt us all.

They had never been taught how to best pursue each other. Neither had ever been asked what it would mean for them to sell out to the idea of making their marriage work.

Neither had ever asked what they would be willing to pay or risk to get what they want out of their marriage.

They had never actually considered what the point of their marriage was or should be.

I told Eric and Emily, "It is my belief that any couple can come back from anything. They simply need to learn how to build the most important ingredient into their relationship and answer some basic questions every day."

THE OTHER SIDE OF PAIN

I've worked with couples who had multiple affairs—with pens ready to sign divorce papers—and they came back from those terrible situations. One husband cheated on his wife with one of her best friends while she was in the hospital with their newborn baby.

Not only are they together today, but they will tell you that they are best friends.

How does that happen?

How does a couple caught in the deepest hurt move from the most significant pain of feeling the widest gulf between them to being best friends? It happens by both individuals being committed to healing and hope. When both people are willing to move toward each other and invite the other person to walk beside them, healing occurs.

But this process is painful. It doesn't feel good. I cannot tell you how many times someone has said to me, "But I don't feel like it should be this hard!" or "I don't feel like I should have to endure this pain."

Eric and Emily both said that to me. I told them the same thing I always say at those moments: "*This hard*" is subjective and they are correct in believing that they do not have to endure the pain. But no matter what they choose to do, there will be pain, especially if kids are involved. And if they want their marriage to work, they have to walk through the pain. One of the biggest lies we allow our brains to tell us is that we do not have a choice in a situation. Whenever people tell me they "shouldn't have to endure pain" or "they don't have to go through the pain," I tell them I agree with them. They can always choose to exclude a particular pain from their life. There is a catch, though.

Everything in life that is worth having is almost always on the other side of pain. By avoiding the thing that scares us, we avoid the things we want to be in our life. We succeed in avoiding one pain only to invite and welcome another pain into our life. There is always pain.

Eric and Emily had what many would consider to be a big problem in their marriage. There was infidelity—emotionally, if not physically—and it was this giant life-sucking hole that permeated every area of their relationship. They had a much bigger problem, though. This giant problem would allow them to ignore the many smaller problems that had led them to this point.

Emily was not being completely honest that day, and there was more to the story (there often is). And Eric had some secrets of his own to share. They were both holding onto their secrets because they had failed to create a safe place to share the hard things about their life.

We all have these traumas in our relationships. Our screw-ups sit in the back corner of our brain, taunting us. They expose our shame and demand we hide it. They bark loudly and obnoxiously until we acquiesce and hide them. In hiding our shame, we hide ourselves.

We retreat our true inner being to the shadows where the shame can grow into its own dragon, seeking to slay us.

Then we try to soothe our pain. We try to soothe it by working out or making millions of dollars or getting involved in church. We try to outdo our shame, falsely believing that we can outrun it through activity. The net result becomes a heaping of shame on top of shame. Our activity does not do away with our shame; instead, it numbs our response to it. A numb soul tends to be numb to everything. This causes us to pick activities that keep us from connecting with someone else, which causes us to experience more shame.

Sometimes, maybe often, we try to deny our shame by simply retreating and not doing anything. This can lead to clinical depression. We keep the blinds in the house down and lose all sense of meaning for life. Our zest fades like the dying light of late autumn.

Most of the time, we strike an uneasy balance between those two extremes and we still fail to heal. Our world spins faster and faster as we scramble to catch up. We don't find satisfaction in what should be our deepest and most significant relationship, all the while failing to realize that one of the biggest contributing factors to a failed marriage is overlooking a truly safe place to be all-in with our whole body.

This book will give you the tools to be able to create such a space for your loved ones. A space where complete safety can grow and blossom. The challenge for you will be engaging your greatest fears as you seek that which you desire the most.

Chapter 2:

Emotional Security Is the Key

Too many people ask the wrong question: "Will my marriage make it?"

I want to know if they'll be glad they made it to the end. Society almost has an expectation that their marriage will not make it—that it is somehow doomed to fail.

I want to fight that perception.

I want people to be excited to be married. I want them to be excited that they stayed together for their entire life. I'm afraid that marriage is becoming the new divorced in our society. When I was a child, divorce was relatively uncommon. It was considered taboo.

Today, we have gone the other way. As with so many things in our society, we seem to lack the ability to be gracious to one group of people without being ungracious to the opposite group. People who are married for a long time are met with jeers and sneers.

Their love is met with disbelief and disdain. I once had a coworker marvel at me reaching my eight-year anniversary. He could not believe that one of us had not had an affair. His exact words were, "I can't imagine having sex with just one person for that long. It has to suck." A few years later, he was going through a divorce with his wife of six months.

As a society, we have come to expect marriages to fail. We have coined the term "throwaway marriage." As in, "Well, my brother just got divorced, but he's only twenty-seven so it's just his throwaway marriage," which I heard once at a party.

I want to change that; I want people to be excited that their marriage made it. To do that, we have to achieve certain milestones in every relationship. While the application of these principles will look differently in every relationship, they all must be present for those relationships to make it and thrive.

What Is the Most Important Thing?

Sometimes, when I go out to eat, I embarrass my family. Well, mostly I embarrass my kids. I love to ask the server one of two questions. And now, I would like to ask you one of those questions. Your answer to this question will impact how you treat other people in your life. Your answer is probably the number-one driving force in how you treat your spouse or how you treat those you love. Even if you are bad at relationships and seem to have one bad relationship after another, your answer to this question could be affecting your life. Your life is probably more shaped by your answer to this question than any other force in your life, even if you don't realize it.

Grab a piece of paper and a pen. Write the answer to my question down on paper. If you get more than one answer, write as many as you can. Whatever comes to mind, just write it down.

What do you think is the single most important quality to making a relationship work? What went through your head? Did something immediately spring to mind? Sometimes, people look at me and say that there is not just one thing, but that there are many things; so I ask them to throw two or three at me. In your case, just write them down on paper.

What came to mind? I have compiled an official list over the years of answers I have received from various people. I've listed a few of them for you below:

- Communication
- Trust
- Common goals/interests
- Common spiritual beliefs
- Love
- Similar ethnic backgrounds
- Passion
- Romance
- Hard work

All of these things are great. On one hand, it is a

fantastic list. A strong relationship will have all of these elements in it. In fact, the healthier the relationship, the more these things will be in the relationship. But— you knew there was one coming, didn't you?—these elements are *not* the most important things. They are important, yes. But there are marriages with all of these things that end up in divorce.

What was your answer? Do you know anyone who has had that "thing," whatever it is, in their relationship and they still ended up divorced? I know someone who had at least one of those characteristics, and yet, their marriage ended in divorce. Sometimes, people focus on communicating and still find that they lack— they're not sure what they lack, but they are certain *something* is lacking.

I have a strong connection with many faith communities. The city I live in is inundated with a high church population. Often, I hear people say that having a similar faith is the key to a satisfying, lasting relationship. Sadly, the numbers do not bear this out. Look them up, and you will find that people inside the church are getting divorced at the same rate as people outside the church. Too many people have told me they loved their spouse but had to get divorced—even if they didn't want to. Love and church do not seem to be a safe insulator against divorce.

Everything on that list leads to one thing and that is the most important quality. I wonder why we take something as emotional as relationships and take emotion out of it. We often try to make relationships a simple sum. I confess, as a marriage counselor, this can be a persnickety trap of activity for me to put in front of my clients. Like most dangerous pitfalls, there is truth to be found here. Our relationships should not and cannot be ruled by emotion, and yet, we must keep emotion at the forefront of our goals.

My answer to the question is *emotional security*. If you have emotional security, you will have a relationship that will not only last but will also thrive. It will be hot and heavy. Some people call this *emotional attachment*, but that is one step away from the home run. Emotional attachment comes after you are *emotionally secure*.

Look back at the list I gave you. They all lead to emotional security. If the relationship is to last, it will move past those things and end up in emotional security. Relationships that do not end up with a high level of emotional security will not last. Things like romance, love, and passion are not on a constant flow. They ebb and flow throughout a lifetime. Sometimes, they will flow hot and heavy. Sometimes, they will ebb slowly and trickle along. It is in these times that the emotional security will act as the glue that holds the relationship together.

The Three Questions We All Want Answered

Have you ever heard, "Most affairs are not about the sex"? It seems so counterintuitive, but it's right.

Certainly, affairs happen for a variety of reasons, but after talking to more cheaters than I care to count, I am convinced that one of the key reasons for the affair is almost always an attempt by someone to feel more emotionally secure. Please hear what I am saying: I am not saying that the person who was cheated on is to blame for the affair. Who we need to blame is always a losing conversation. What I am trying to get at is the *reason* for the affair.

In a later chapter, we will talk about sex, but let me discuss it briefly here first. You can have really hot and heavy sex without being emotionally secure for a time. If you don't believe me, go to a local high school hallway. Talk to some college students. Young people are having sex and often it is temporarily fulfilling sex. It is hard to be emotionally secure with your spouse and have boring sex. Guys, if you are having a hard time getting your wife to want sex, it is probably because she does not feel emotionally secure with you. If you don't believe me, go ask her how emotionally secure she feels. Be prepared for an answer you might not like. This is the first place I start when a couple comes to me with an unhappy sex life. We almost never have to go anywhere else.

Our level of emotional security is directly determined by the answers we find to three core questions:

Question 1: Am I being heard? Specifically, are you actively listening to what I am saying? Are you hearing the words and examining my body language so that you can better understand what I am trying to communicate even if I can't find the words? If you want to convince me that you are not hearing me, just interrupt me and tell me how to fix the problem before I am done talking (guys, I am not trying to pick on us here, but we are terrible at this business). There is something cathartic and healing in being heard.

Question 2: Am I valued? Not just for what I do, but for who I am. Do you find intrinsic worth in me? Do you find time to be with me? Am I high on your priority list? Am I more important than Sunday afternoon football? Am I more important that shopping with the girls? Where do I fit in your priority list? Am I more important to you than the feeling you get when you are angry with me so you avoid saying hurtful things? If you want to convince me that I am not valued, just ignore me. Don't find time to talk to me. Of course, don't find time to hear me, and you can give me two nos at one time.

How much of our various youth culture movements are an attempt to be heard and to be valued? When a young man pulls up next to me and his stereo system is so loud that it reverberates through my car, I cannot help but wonder if he is just asking to be heard—I wonder if he is asking if I will value him. When someone covers his or her body in various tattoos or piercings, I wonder if he or she isn't simply trying to be heard and valued. How much of our attempts to stand out (usually by fitting in) are simply attempts at being valued?

Question 3: Am I safe to share? If you hear me and you seem to place some value in me, but I cannot trust you, I will not be emotionally secure with you. If you trust me and I judge you or use what you share with me in moments of anger (think of couples fighting), you are not going to be emotionally secure with our relationship. And like a tree that needs space, sunshine, and water to grow, our relationship needs all three of these as well. Take one away, and the tree may grow a little bit, but it will not grow to full capacity. Many times, it will wither and die. Emotional safety is the nourishment that keeps being heard and valued to grow into an emotionally secure relationship.

THE KEY TO A HEALTHY RELATIONSHIP

I met Susan because of a wound.

Not a physical wound, but one that was even more insidious. She never felt safe to emotionally share her entire life with anyone. At age nine, she was sexually assaulted. Her father told she was worthless all of her life. She was emotionally tormented by her husband for nearly twenty years. She vacillated between hating herself for being beautiful and hating herself for not being beautiful enough. Susan once told me she was sick of men telling her she was beautiful—she wanted a man who wanted more than a one-night stand. She was willing to go through hours of plastic surgery and spend more money than some people will spend on a house to make her body look a certain way. She didn't do this because she loved her husband, but because she thought that might be the final thing that would cause her husband to love her.

Do you think Susan ever shared her dreams with her husband? If she felt that she had to go through all of that just to *maybe* cause him to love her, do you think she ever felt truly valued or heard? Is it any wonder that she finally contemplated suicide? Would you be shocked if I told you that she had three children who were all very angry? How good do you think Dad was at answering these core questions for them? Of course, the obvious question is how would he have been a different dad and husband if he had the three core questions answered for him by people in his life?

The one thing we need is emotional security. But what is it? So far, I have told you that we need one thing and then told you that we have three core questions. So, is it one or three? The answer is yes. Emotional security goes beyond emotional attachment. Emotional security is essential because it will glue you and your spouse together.

If you have ever seen a person who inspires loyalty in the people that work for her, you have seen someone who knows how to create emotional security in other people. Emotional security comes from being able to answer all three core questions in the affirmative. I believe we are hardwired to get these answers from our parents when we are children. If you're a parent, you will answer this question for your child. More than anyone else, you will form the emotional security your child will have as an adult. If you can answer these core questions for them as a child and a teenager, it will set them up for life. Of course, when they get married, they will want to find emotional security in their relationship with their partner. What they learn from you regarding emotional security will help them give it to their spouse and their own children.

Of course, your children will also learn emotional security from how you and your spouse interact with each other. You are responsible for creating fertile ground for emotional security in your spouse. It is paramount for you to understand that you cannot grow it in your spouse, but you can and must create the opportunity for your spouse's emotional security to grow. In many instances, you will be working against growth killers planted in the emotional heart of your spouse over the years. A person who grew up believing that she cannot trust others with anything but *that one thing* is not going to suddenly trust her spouse with it simply because they are married. Factor in the divorce rates and to many people, it only seems prudent that they would not share *everything* with a person who may or may not be there in the end.

If you are married, your mission is to tend to the soul and heart of your spouse in a way that offers opportunity for them to trust you with the seeds of emotional security. You get to pull the weeds that others have planted. You get to prepare the soil and plant the seed. You get to water the seeds and provide sunshine. But you must wait for it to grow.

My wife and I have planted gardens in the past. Some gardens have been an abject failure, and some have seen a modicum of success. No matter the results, could you imagine if we planted our garden and then became angry because we did not see any results the same day? Would you laugh any less at us if we became angry over a lack of results a week later? How about two weeks? Of course, we think that would be silly. The analogy breaks down a little bit when we move it over to human relationships. Of course, even in gardens there is an end time. We know that eventually the corn will grow and if it does not grow, something is wrong and we need to fix it.

Human relationships do not come with any such known timetable. I could try to sell a lot of books by saying that I have finally figured it out and if you would just do these seven things, your spouse would have emotional security with you in seven short weeks. It would work as well as the next diet fad. I do know if you are doing the things that cultivate fertile ground for emotional security, eventually your spouse will start to move toward a healthy place of being emotionally secure. It may take some individualized counseling. It may take longer than you or even your spouse would like for it to take, but it will happen.

ARE YOU EMOTIONALLY NAKED?

Knowing that you need to get to something does not mean you know what exactly it is or how to get there. I imagine you might be sitting there, wondering, "What exactly is emotional security? How do we get it?" This question is vitally important as we seek to figure out how to have the relationship we have always wanted, hoped, and dreamed we could have.

Emotional security is knowing that it is safe to know and be known. It is knowing that it is okay to be emotionally naked.

We spend so much of our life hiding. Most people are so afraid that they will be found out. That they will be found out to be dreamers, artists, lovers—you can fill almost anything here. As humans, we learn very early in life that our dreams are to be kept secret. We learn that people will laugh when we share from the deepest parts of our heart. We long to find someone we can truly know and whom we can trust to truly know us. We long to find someone we can give ourselves to completely. This is why sex is never just sex. We're never more intimate when we are lying naked next to someone completely exposed.

Sharon knew exactly what I was talking about when I brought up this idea to her. Her tears flowed freely as we discussed her relationship with her husband. Married for almost twelve years, from the outside things seemed good in their relationship. She sobbed as she told me that no one knew there were any problems in their relationship. "Our kids are great. We live in an awesome neighborhood and we make a great living. I'm just... I'm just tired of living with a roommate."

Jack didn't feel all that different from Sharon. He just hid it behind, "Everything's fine. I don't know why she wants to be here. We don't fight much, except when *I screw up!* Just ask her, she'll tell you."

I looked at them and suggested that while their life was fairly normal, they were missing emotional security. Sharon vigorously shook her head as I suggested that Jack hid behind his humor and antics to stay safe. Jack eyed me suspiciously as I suggested that Sharon used brute verbal force to do the same thing. They were stuck. The very things that made Sharon feel safe made Jack feel unsafe—and vice versa. Unless they found a way to change the way they interacted, they would probably remain stuck until they either divorced or died bitter with each other.

I do not believe that is an overstatement. We all know too many people who have made it. They have stayed married. But they fight every day. They are bitter with each other and the world. They walk around with a metaphorical suit of jet fuel tied to their body and emotions. The smallest spark from their spouse and that fuel is set on fire, erupting in hurtful words that leave deep scars. Because everyone knows these types of couples, I often hear people say, "That's why I got divorced, because I couldn't spend the rest of my life being unhappy."

But second marriages don't have much of a better track record than first marriages. In fact, statistically they fail at a much higher rate. There are still problems to deal with. There are still issues to be navigated. The issue is we don't know how to build emotional equity. For Jack and Sharon, their initial thought of their spouse was almost always negative.

Do you remember when you were dating your spouse? Do you remember how you would think about them and a spontaneous smile would come across your face? You could spend hours with them and when you were done, thinking of them would still bring a smile to your face.

Then you got married. Life kicked in as you had children to care for, bills to pay, and responsibilities to gather. You lost your time where you built your relational equity. Do you remember fighting or having a disagreement when you were dating? When it was over, how long did it take to *be* over? With most couples, it takes very little time at all. When the narrative of one's story begins to fall apart, it takes a lot longer for a fight to be over. Why? Because you've come to that place where your thoughts about your partner and your relationship are mostly unhappy thoughts. At this point, when you have a fight, it stews in your brain for days. Even if you try to avoid the circle of conflict (more on that later) and pretend something doesn't bother you, you have moved from actively treasuring your spouse to actively trying *not* to think about your spouse. Essentially, you are treasuring the absence of conflict. The absence of conflict is not peace. Someone once said that where our treasure goes, that is where our heart will also go.

This is backward to our way of thinking. We believe we should have feelings and then we will value and treasure our spouse. It's our responsibility to build relational equity into our spouse. When we do loving things for our spouse, we find that our love for our spouse will increase and our tolerance for their misdeeds will grow. Doing loving things for them helps us to love them.

To become courageous, we must do courageous things. To develop love, we must do loving things. We build our own emotional equity.

If you want your relationship to improve, you cannot look to your spouse to fix it. Yes, your spouse wanting to change will be part of the equation, but you need to understand that first and foremost, *you must change*. If your relationship is in trouble, it is because you both have probably stopped building emotional security.

You cannot change your spouse. You can only change yourself.

Chapter 3:

The Power of Relational Equity

MY WIFE AND I ARE BOTH MENTAL HEALTH therapists, and we both do marriage and relationship conferences together. The truth is that she is probably the best therapist in the house. This will often lead people to ask me what our fights are like. I've actually had someone ask me if I would be willing to videotape one. I politely declined. Once, I had a friend ask me about it. I told him it is rare for us to have a fight. We have plenty of conflict, but we rarely have fights. You know the kind. The kind where the roof comes off the house from the internal fireworks or the windows break from the deep freeze that kicks off where neither partner talks to each other for days. Emotionally destructive verbal bombs get lobbed indiscriminately across the landscape of your relationship without any thought for tomorrow. We just never have them.

Until, one day we did. It was the night before my

friend asked me about our fights.

I told him, "It's funny you ask. Despite the fact that we rarely have them, we had a pretty serious fight just last night."

My friend said, "Now you gotta pay."

I replied, "No, not really. We both apologized and owned our own mistakes. It's over now." He didn't believe me. I assured him I wasn't lying to him. It truly was over. We would probably joke about it for a while, but the actual fighting part was over. No more emotional damage.

The obvious question is how does a couple get there? I think everyone can get there. They need to work on their relational equity. You do that by living by your vows. You remember those? Those pesky promises to love your spouse more than anyone else, including yourself?

What happens when we live that way? We build relational equity. When your spouse knows you're upset or hurt and you purposely choose loving words, you build relational equity. When your spouse knows you purposely work at your communication skills, you build relational equity. There is a myriad of ways to build equity. We will not touch on all of them in this book, but any time you put your spouse and the health of your relationship ahead of your own desires, you build equity. It's like making a deposit into a bank.

In the same way, every time you throw a temper tantrum or act childish, you chip away at your relational equity. You make a withdrawal. When you try to manipulate your spouse into doing what you want them to do (either through punishment)—"I'm not talking to him/her"—or reward—"Jim just knows that if he wants sex, he better do what I want him to do"—we are chipping away at the well of relational equity our spouse has stored up for us.

We also add to our own equity. Sounds ridiculous, doesn't it? Telling your wife you love her will increase your love for her. If you don't want to have sex with your husband, you should because that will increase your desire to have sex with him.

Relational equity occurs when we build into the relationship.

STOP MANIPULATING

Stop attempting to manipulate your spouse into doing what you want them to do. In fact, you can never manipulate someone into doing something and have a long-term healthy relationship with them. Seriously, think about the people you know: how many of them had manipulation as a part of their story and it went well? How many of them ended in divorce?

One of the sad truths of being a counselor is that people are resistant to the idea of changing their own behavior to change the relationship. Every time you manipulate, even if you get what you wanted, you lose relational equity. If your relational equity hits zero, you destroy emotional security. It's that simple.

Our view of our relationship is not made in a day. Our spouse's view of the painting that is our relationship is not made in a day. It's a compilation of a thousand brushstrokes. Those brushstrokes either build or take down relational equity. We make large deposits or withdrawals in the arena of conflict with our spouse. Think about how many hurtful things are said in a fight. Consider how often you speak over your partner simply to tell him that he's wrong before he has even had the chance to articulate his thoughts. How many times have you felt that he was implying you were stupid and that he was failing to listen to you because you were trying to express your feelings? This is the pattern we must change. We must change it in how we fight, how we communicate, and how we do life together.

If you're a yeller and you purposely don't yell, your spouse can't help but notice. If you are a sarcasmer (yes, I made up that word) and you refrain from using sarcasm, your partner will take notice. If you are a shutdown withdrawer and you purposely engage... well, I think you get the idea.

It will be messy. Life is messy. Love is messy. When we enter into a marriage relationship, we are trying to build both. It's bound to be incredibly messy, but also worth it. The problem is that usually we expect our spouse to notice and respond immediately. We expect the equity to build in one shot. The yeller doesn't yell, and his spouse still attacks. That's it! Back to yelling for him.

Imagine buying a house and then being angry because the equity didn't go up significantly the next day. That would be ridiculous and most people would laugh at a person who reacted that way. But that is exactly what people do when they get upset because their spouses didn't notice that they'd changed after one or two disagreements, or even after multiple disagreements.

FOCUS ON THE POSITIVES

If you are fighting with your spouse a lot, you're probably focusing on the negatives. Let's say that your husband has been promising to get something done in the backyard for months. You keep bringing it up and he doesn't do it! Finally, you resort to little comments. Still no movement on the project!

This was exactly the case with Davi and Denise. Denise needed a fort built for the kids in the backyard, and Davi had said that he would do it but never did.

When I asked Denise if she knew why Davi wouldn't do it, she said that she didn't but she assumed it was because it wasn't as important to him as it was to her. I looked at Davi and asked him if this were true. He told me that it was not true. He believed the fort needed to be built as much as Denise thought it needed to be built.

41

This left two other potential reasons. First, Davi felt inadequate to build the fort. If this were true, I was going to have a rough road in front of me to get any traction on this issue. We tend to avoid the areas where we feel inadequate as though they are plague-producing. In truth, I didn't think this was the issue for Davi. He was a very competent carpenter.

The second possibility was Davi figured that Denise would tear his building apart. She would find things she didn't like about it and complain. She would move from one negative to another, and then she would eventually complain about the next project that he wasn't going to do. In Davi's mind, there was no pay-off to building this fort because it would end badly.

When Davi thought about doing something for Denise, his immediate thought was that it would go badly. This is an example of negative equity. Denise had driven her equity account to zero by constantly complaining about everything he did.

After confirming that I was correct about my assumption, I asked him for an example, as Denise was escalating her voice to ask for some examples herself.

"Sure," he said. "Last Christmas, I built some storage for the boys. It took me three days. She didn't like the stain I used. This past spring, I made new doors for the shed, but she didn't like the design for the doors. Two weeks ago, she yelled at me because I put the dogs outside (in a heated pen) for the *whole day*!"

As he was giving each example, she rolled her eyes

and at first denied, then dismissed his thoughts.

"Oh. My. Word," she said with a heavy punctuation between each word. "Do you really think those things are me saying I don't like your work?"

Finally, she dismissed his thoughts by saying, "I didn't say that I didn't like the doors. I just didn't think it was your best work. You are just too darn sensitive. You need to build a little gumption into your backbone!"

He looked at me with plaintive eyes and said, "See?"

Both Davi and Denise had stopped building relational equity into their lives. I asked Denise what she thought would happen if she just said thank you and praised Davi when he built the fort. She laughed and said, "He'd probably pass out."

I asked Davi what he thought would happen if he just built it and then made the changes that Denise brought up afterward. He laughed and said, "I'd be at it forever."

That's the part I can't deny. Intentionally building relational equity takes time. It's long. But then again, so is fighting. Divorce is expensive, both financially and emotionally. Instead of being around to hear his wife's comments, Davi just bailed. He went fishing. He went to his buddy's house to work on their race car.

Those actions made him feel temporarily safe. But they made him feel completely insecure in the long run. He focused on the negatives, and he lost.

So did Denise. She focused on what Davi *didn't* do.

She failed to focus on what he *did* do. Consequently, he did less. Because they both refused to build into the relationship, it withered. It shrank to the point where they felt like strangers when they were around each other. They fought about everything. Any afternoon might look like the following scenario:

She'd ask him to fold clothes.

He'd fold the clothes.

She'd complain because he didn't do it the way she wanted him to.

So, he stopped folding the clothes.

Then she complained because he stopped folding the clothes.

She asked him to clean the house.

He did.

Because he cleaned the house, he figured she'd want to have sex.

She didn't want to have sex.

He became angry because she didn't want to have sex, and then blustered and yelled.

Now she really didn't want to have sex.

That is a common pattern to a relationship where relational equity has been lost. But it doesn't have to be that way. A couple doesn't have to be stuck in a pattern of *doing* to *get*. Couples must commit to the idea of giving without expecting anything in return. But that goes directly against why we got into the relationship in the first place. Most of us got into our relationship for what we were getting out of it. It's easy to see how this creates problems for us in the future. How often have you heard someone say, "I love being with so-and-so because of how great I am when I am with her"?

Committing to loving the other person regardless of what they do builds relational equity. It's also probably the hardest thing you will ever try to do. When relationships are stuck in a particularly nasty and severely negative narrative, the heart of each partner is as numb as if it has been encased in ice. Layer upon layer of ice. Each act of love—that doesn't come with an expectation in return—is an attempt to melt that ice just a little bit at a time.

That's the rub, isn't it? An act of love done with an expectation of return isn't love.

Folding clothes expecting to get sex isn't love.

Cooking dinner expecting to get a foot rub isn't love.

Love must be given without an expectation of return. Love has to be free in order to be love. It comes without guile or a price. But when we try to repair relationships that have little to no relational equity, we tend to do just that. We demand love be recognized. We give love, but we want it to be lauded and recompensed.

The minute that happens, it stops being love and starts becoming a *transaction*. It is no longer love. It is something less. It is often hurtful and continues the cycle of pain, fights, and exasperation. Relational equity is built by giving love without expecting anything in return.

THE PROBLEM IS THE WORD *EVENTUALLY*

A common pushback I get on this idea is that it seems nearly impossible and it could set a person up to be in a bad position for a long time. I mean, who's going to do something and not expect anything in return? That's why it's a paradox. The husband who commits to loving his wife no matter what, for as long as it takes, will often win her over… eventually. The wife who commits to loving her husband regardless of how he acts for as long as it takes will eventually melt the ice around his heart.

One of the biggest factors in the ice not melting is the truth that we don't usually give it time. We take years to build up hurts, wounds, and scars that all coalesce into this numb, frozen blob of ice called an emotional heart. Then we get mad when it doesn't change in days or weeks. We need a renewal of the words *commitment* and *endurance*.

We have to stop thinking that we have to feel something in order to do it. This is patently false in almost every other area of our life. We don't always feel like going to work, but we do. Why? Because we want that paycheck. The idea that we have to *want* to do something in order to do it is really a terrible way to live our lives. There are many things we force ourselves to do before it becomes something we want to do.

Allowing yourself to believe the insidious lie that you must want to be loving with your spouse before you will act loving toward them enslaves you to a fate that is almost guaranteed. You are removing the possibility of changing from the equation. You are saying that your feelings are the supreme dictator of your actions.

Think about this with children. Would you allow your children to throw a temper tantrum simply because they *felt like it*? You expect your children to act in a certain manner despite how they feel. This ability is key to a marriage turning around from a negative and destructive narrative to a healthy and positive one. You must be willing to approach your spouse in a way that is completely loving, despite how you feel. This intentionality builds relational equity because it tells your spouse that you are someone who can be trusted. It tells them that you care about the relationship first and foremost. When they truly believe this, they know you are going to do what is best for the both of you.

When we build relational equity, we create a space where bad things can happen but not define the relationship. We create space for a fight to occur and no one has to pay. We move back to a time when differences were celebrated.

Do you remember that time? Probably when you were dating, you celebrated the differences between you and your spouse. Whatever was different was cute and adorable and proof that you were meant to be. If you're caught in a bad narrative, those same differences are now lamented.

If you're not caught in a bad narrative but want

to improve your relationship, you still need to consider being intentional to build relational equity. Why? Because relational equity is either growing or shrinking—there is rarely an in-between. When we have relational equity, we can go through a fight because the anger associated with our fights is filtered through the lens of wanting to protect the relationship and the heart and soul of our partner. The fight is a scene in a chapter but not the whole story of our relationship.

Relational equity must be built intentionally. You must control your tongue when you are talking to your spouse. When you are in a stressful moment, you must control what you say, how you say it, and how you hear what is said.

To be healthy, a person must control how they hear what is said. This doesn't mean that you should act as though you didn't hear what they said. It means you make sure that you know what they said before you respond. Think about how many arguments you've had because you answered a question before you knew the question being asked. Later in this book, I'm going to teach you some simple communication techniques that can transform your relationship. They are simple but not easy. They will build equity in your relationship. Communication is not the only way to build relational equity, but it is one of the biggest ways to do it.

Before we get into any other area of how relational equity, and thus emotional security, is built, we need to look at a foundational beginning. That foundation is your assumptions of the other person. When you hear what your spouse is saying, do you interpret it through the lens of a generous assumption or a cynical assumption? Do you try to see it in the best possible light or do you default to the worst possible interpretation?

So much of interpretation is about our own focus, our own lens. I am amazed at how often people will consistently assume the worst about someone with whom they have decided to raise children and spend their rest of their life together. When we start with a positive assumption, it allows room for us to explore with our partner what they meant without raising defensiveness. It allows us to let them know that we love and trust them while maybe not agreeing with them.

How Is Relational Equity Built?

There is a myriad of ways that couples can build equity into their relationship. Being intentional with their time is certainly one of them. Spending a quantity of time together is important. I know we often hear that quality matters more than quantity and for a season of life, I agree with that. Certainly, there are times when we have to limit the amount of time we can spend together. But over the long haul for most couples, quantity will be just as important as quality.

A great exercise to do is ask your spouse, "What

can I do to build equity into our relationship? What are the things I could do that help you know I love you and value our relationship?" The trick is to *do* those things. For Danielle earlier in the chapter, it was helping her with chores around the house. For my wife, it's listening. Doing things that cause the person to be heard, valued, and safe builds equity into a relationship.

What I'm *Not* Saying

I can already hear some guy saying, "See, you have to stay with me no matter what I do!" No, you don't. You can choose to leave. If he's hitting you, leave. Leave right now. Come back to this book. But leave. If your children are being hit, leave. If your partner is flaunting their affairs, leave. If they have an addiction that is terrorizing your family, leave.

You don't have to live with someone to commit to love them unconditionally. People who are being abused should leave. They do not have to live in that hell. Sometimes, it is the cold wakeup call of someone saying, "That's it, you can't do this anymore" that causes people to actually change. I cannot say this strongly enough: *if you are in danger, leave.*

Chapter 4:

How Do We Get to a Healthy Relationship?

HOW DO PEOPLE CHANGE? THAT'S THE REAL question when it comes to how we build a strong, lasting relationship.

Our world can be broken down in many different ways. I find the following to be one of the most helpful ways to understand life—both my own and the lives of those I love. I believe this is important because it breaks us down in a way that allows us to effect change.

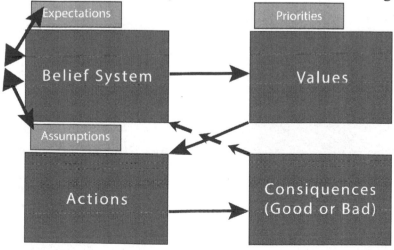

BELIEF SYSTEM AND VALUES

I am going to look at the top two boxes first: the belief system and the values. These two boxes are contained in your mind. I cannot see them just by looking at you. I cannot look at you and say, "He values exercise." I have to see the bottom two boxes—actions and consequences—because they can be seen in the physical world. We will look at actions and consequences in the next chapter.

BELIEF SYSTEM

We all have a belief system. It runs everything in your life. Every decision in your life about how something should be, or the quality of something, starts in this spot. Our belief system drives the bus of our lives.

Our belief system is comprised by things we take as truth without much debate. They are settled in our minds (politics, current hot-button issues, religion). The answers to those questions are all formed in your belief system.

I live in West Michigan, home of many churches and Amway. Often, when I explain this concept to people here, I ask them to tell me the first two things that enter their mind when I bring those two institutions up. Whatever their answer is, it gives me an insight into their belief system. Many people have cynical views of both institutions.

Our culture highly affects our belief system. When you meet a new person, do you shake their hand? Do you kiss them on the cheek? Whatever you do, that action is a result of your belief system.

When I was a kid, I grew up rural and poor. I went to a private, somewhat affluent undergraduate university. It was an interesting mix that would have probably given some social scientist a lot of wonderful material to sift through. One of the cultural differences was clothing. I grew up believing that anything with a collar on was dressing up.

T-shirts were the daily dress, and church dress-up could be a simple polo. Not so with many of my dorm mates. Their casual dress was the polo shirt. This didn't cause much conflict, because I could adjust and because many people just didn't care what I wore.

There is one clear example that I remember from college when differing belief systems were present. My sophomore year, I met a girl. I wanted to impress her so I started dressing up. In those days, my school had a dress code for underclassmen and upperclassmen, but they were not the same. My freshman year, I skirted the dress code. For instance, I was supposed to wear a collar to every class and the occasional school sweatshirt. I wore a school sweatshirt almost every day and rarely wore a collar. I was supposed to wear dress pants and the occasional colored jeans but no blue jeans. I wore colored jeans every day and rarely dressed up.

My sophomore year, I started wearing the dress

code for upperclassmen. I did this, not because I was more invested in the school's dress code or because I bought into the school's system, but because I wanted to impress a girl. My belief system had not changed; my values had changed. I found something I wanted more than comfort (and maybe the self-satisfaction that came with sticking it to the administration). I went along with the system to gain something (the girl's affection), but that gain came with a cost. One that I decided I couldn't tolerate.

I was walking into an all-school assembly when a girl said to me, "Wow, you must really be maturing." I looked at her a bit nonplussed. "Well, look at you. You're wearing a tie almost every day now and you are early to chapel (our all-school assembly). Good for you. I'm happy for you—keep it up."

She knew nothing about me but what I wore. We hadn't talked in almost two years. The only thing she could base this statement from was her observation of what I was wearing. Her belief system had an inherent expectation and assumption that mature people wore a certain style of clothing.

I never wore a tie again until I was forced to do so by the system and even then, I worked hard to find ways around the issue. My belief system at the time was that I wasn't going to be branded. For certain, my belief system involved a bit of rebellion as well.

In fact, my time at my undergraduate school was painful for many reasons, but the underlying reason was that I chose poorly in picking a school that had a similar belief system to mine. To be fair, I was picking at eighteen and what do you know at eighteen? Also, from a distance, the school's belief system and mine appeared to be a great match. I was too immature to understand at the time that they didn't match at all and I had missed the clear signs.

Whatever your belief system is, it is important to understand this is the place where your assumptions and expectations are formed. These assumptions and expectations are not always correct. In fact, they may often be wrong, but their accuracy is irrelevant to how you utilize them. Your assumptions and expectations drive the rest of your life.

This is why diets do not work. Diets attempt to change the consequences without changing the assumptions or expectations that drive them. A person who eats comfort food isn't going to see improvement because the diet is attempting to change actions without changing assumptions and expectations.

In other words, the diet is attempting to fix the problem by going after the wrong box. Until the individual can deal with the underlying belief that they need to consume food to be comforted, they will not find success in their weight loss journey.

Sometimes, we act in a way that is directly contradictory to our belief system. This is non-integrated living, or having a lack of integrity. One of the biggest problems that I encounter in this arena is people's false belief about authenticity. We seem to believe that if we feel something, we have to act on it. This is the exact opposite of what we teach our children when they are young, but somewhere over time, we morph in our thinking.

This thinking kills relationships. Too many people think that authenticity is doing what I *feel*. Authenticity is doing what is *best* and *right*. The problem with the former ideation regarding authenticity is it is fraught with opportunities to do selfish and wrong things. Furthermore, it devalues doing the right thing for the sake of doing the right thing.

Think back to Eric and Emily. When Eric first had confirmation of the affair, do you think he wanted to stay in the relationship? I know for a fact he did not. He wanted to leave. Do you think Emily wanted to go through the shame of revealing details? Do you think she wanted to give the details of her failings? Do you think Eric wanted to hear how his own failings had led to him being wronged in one of the worst possible situations? I promise you the answer was no. This is one of the biggest problems that keeps couples apart.

They can't engage in real guilt and healing because they mistakenly believe it will hinder their authenticity. However, the truth is that they misunderstand authenticity. Authenticity is not acting true to my feelings; it is acting true to my belief system and the values that come from it.

Authenticity will be extremely painful and healing.

I often tell couples that whatever they decide to do (work it out or get divorced) will be painful because that is simply how it works.

If I am going to help them move forward to a place of healing, I must challenge their belief system because all their assumptions come from that place.

One of the biggest problems I often hear is the statement: "This just shouldn't be this hard." That is a classic belief system statement. It is an assumption that if the relationship is hard, it must not be right. This is a broken and untrue belief, but it drives the actions nevertheless.

This is why our belief system is so important and yet it seems to me that it often gets the least amount of thought. We create and develop both our expectations and assumptions about life and what will happen in life.

Take for instance, a couple where one has an expectation that sex will be part of their life regardless of how they are doing emotionally, and the other believes that they should only have sex when they are doing well. This couple is set up for failure, unless they can find a way to articulate what they are thinking, process what the other person is thinking, and then come to an appropriate compromise.

Think about the girl from my college days. She had an expectation that people who were maturing into adulthood wore dressier clothes. When we try to diminish or downplay our expectations and what we believe, we cause more problems because we lie to everyone (including ourselves) about what we believe and want. Meanwhile, the actual beliefs are still running our lives. Those beliefs are creating expectations and wants. Our dishonesty creates confusion and anxiety for the people in our life.

The most powerful lies are the ones that we tell ourselves. When we refuse to acknowledge our belief system, everything else runs amok. Add social pressure to believe a certain way, and we have a perfect recipe for a mess.

Consider the wife I was once talking to about her expectations regarding her husband. I asked her if she would be okay with him going to a local bar for a few drinks after work with female coworkers. Her response was absolutely, if he was in a group. I asked her if she would be bothered if he was alone with the female coworker. She responded in a beautifully honest way and told me that she wanted to say it wouldn't be a problem, but inside she felt it would bother her. She was afraid to say it would be a problem because she was afraid her spouse or her friends would shame her for not trusting him or for being a prude.

Now, think about how this would have played out in real life if she had moved forward with telling her husband it would not be a problem. If he had gone to the local bar for a drink with the female coworker thinking that his wife was okay with it, he would have gone home thinking that they were in a good spot.

But, when he got home, she would have been irritated and frustrated. For this illustration, let's just say that her favorite coping mechanism was being passive-aggressive. In her frustration, she started dropping these little statements here and there. He might have been dumbfounded and asked her if something was wrong.

And this is where our dishonesty traps us. She could not answer truthfully because she told him the exact opposite just a few hours ago so she tells him that nothing is wrong.

As time passed, he became angry and frustrated. He pulled out his favorite coping mechanism and started being snappy with her.

You can see how they will follow this spiraling pattern into a destructive fight.

If you want to know more about your belief system, what kind of responses were in your head when you were reading about my friend's story regarding after-work drinks?

Some of you were probably thinking she had a problem and some of you were probably thinking that the problem was him. Maybe you were in between those two ends. Whatever you felt and whatever the voice in your head was saying, it is a good indicator regarding your own belief system.

That belief system is important because it creates our assumptions and expectations. Those expectations and assumptions influence each other and are interchangeable. They are the catalyst that starts and moves the entire system.

Assumptions drive everything. We have them and respond to them every day without even thinking about it. It's the result of a closed system. Whatever we assume about a situation will greatly impact our decisions, especially regarding how we respond in relationships.

I have a friend who was deeply hurt by his ex-wife. As long as I have known him, he has sabotaged every relationship since that divorce. Even non-romantic ones. Why? Because he assumes that if he makes himself vulnerable again in a relationship, he will be hurt. He further assumes that pain will be more than he can bear. So, he lives a lonely life. Oh, he fills it with wild, spur-of-the-moment adventures and puts those adventures on Facebook for all to see, but he's lonely. I know because I've asked and in his rawest moments of honesty, he told me about the loneliness.

His assumptions are keeping him from living the life he wants because they are fear-driven. Later, we'll talk about guilt, shame, and fear and the role they play in destroying relationships, but for now just contemplate my friend's life. The only thing he wants is to have someone to love him, but he also wants to feel safe.

He assumes the very thing he wants is potentially too dangerous to possess. Therefore, he runs and hides and obscures, and then draws close to someone (let's be honest, who wants to be alone?). Eventually, he realizes how close he is to someone and he withdraws.

This withdrawal causes pain to the other person, who sooner or later concludes that they cannot trust my friend. His assumptions are now creating assumptions for them.

Those assumptions create expectations. Take my friend Dawn for instance. She assumes that almost everyone she meets is not trustworthy and wants something from her that she can't afford to give them. From the outside, she has a lot of friends, but she will tell you that she has very few close friends. She told me how she struggles when someone is nice to her, wondering what it is the other person wants from her. She finds it difficult to believe that someone could want nothing beyond being friends with her. Now, that doesn't make her wrong. If you are sitting there thinking that sounds awful, it simply means you have a different set of expectations than my friend. That's fine if the two of you don't get married.

What about you? What are your expectations for your relationship? Look at your relationships that cause you the most stress and frustration. Most people seem to think their frustration in life comes from their actions. I believe it actually comes from their belief system. You and the person who is causing you stress have different assumptions and expectations about what should be happening in your relationship.

Sometimes, we have the same assumptions, but we

fail to act in a way that is true to those assumptions and expectations. We are still acting out of our assumptions and expectations—we've just failed to identify the ones that are driving us. For instance, sometimes, we say that we want something when in reality we *want to want* something.

I had a friend who has told me many times how he wants to get in shape by eating better, drinking less, and exercising more. But in the time that I have known him, he has never disciplined himself to do any of those things. I believe it is because he *wants to want* to do those things, but there are other wants that are above them in his priority list.

Let's create an imaginary friend and call her Tracy. Let's say that Tracy has a decent job writing for a local newspaper. She lives in a small town and everyone knows her. She has a generous salary and modest benefits. Most importantly, she has a steady paycheck. One day, a friend calls her up and tells her about a job that they would like to offer her doing freelance work. It's a long-term project that pays well, but there is a chance it could fail.

Tracy turns it down.

Six months later, she is bored out of her mind and struggling with the fact that she chose wrong. She moans that she wants adventure and to be free of her boring life in small-town USA.

If you were truly her friend, you would point out that Tracy doesn't actually want adventure; she *wants to want* it. I know this is confusing and somewhat hard to hear, but Tracy needs to know that she is 100 percent in control of her life. She chose safety and a steady paycheck over adventure because that is what she currently wants.

It might change. It might evolve. But right now, that is what Tracy wants. Denying that truth won't change it. The most powerful lies are the ones that we tell ourselves. Ultimately, Tracy must decide what she wants more: security or adventure.

Often, we end up trapped by our own words. We tell ourselves that we would change if we *could* change, we would move if we *could* move, we would do this or that if we *could* do this or that—as if the power to do those things is being denied us by some outside force.

> *I would go to college if it weren't so expensive.*
> *I would volunteer at a shelter if the people weren't so violent.*
> *I would start a business if I knew it wouldn't fail.*
> *I would risk being vulnerable if my spouse weren't so mean in the past.*

The excuses continue and they sound so believable in one's head. When I work with spouses who have cheated, I find that they often play this game. They say to me, "I've had such-and-such style of relationship with this person over here, but my spouse doesn't know and I don't want to tell him because I don't want to hurt him." That sounds so nice.

But it is nothing more than cow excrement.

What they are doing is trying to avoid their own pain that would come from telling their spouse. They do not want to face the consequences of their choices. They wish to avoid the pain that will come from being found out and being held accountable. They have already hurt their spouse.

It falls apart when run through the lens of assumptions. They are taking their assumptions lens and considering the future. They are realizing that things are things are good enough right now. If they tell their spouse about the relationship, they will cause themselves pain and the relationship status will move to bad.

They assume they can get away with it and that they can somehow come out of it looking like a good, supportive spouse. You might be thinking, "Now, hold on, Joe—the spouse will be caused pain, not the person talking to you."

My assumption (and often the assumption of the person who committed the affair) is that the spouse will be hurt and then angry and then bad consequences will come for the person talking to me. They might get thrown out of the house. They might get divorced. They might lose their marriage. They might be shamed. They might be exposed for being selfish.

Ultimately, their assumptions are about themselves. As you might imagine, this is often a bitter pill to swallow and the person I'm talking to will throw up walls like an ancient city fortifying defenses to hold back the threatening idea that telling their spouse could be beneficial.

I have many assumptions and experiences to support those assumptions that telling their spouse may be the best way for them to find a healthy relationship. Often, my belief frightens the people I'm talking with about what could, indeed, what *should* happen when they talk to their spouse, whom they have wronged. Their fears create different expectations that drive their actions forward. Those fears are based on assumptions––they are shaped from a belief about what *might* or *could happen*. They are not based on fact. They are often steeped in dishonesty.

Assumptions are important because they drive over our values and direct our actions. Often, we spend copious amounts of time trying to dissect our actions or our consequences and we rarely look at what assumptions created those actions and consequences. Therefore, we are often stuck in a pattern of wanting to change but not achieving change. We have to alter the thoughts running through our head before we can alter the rest of our life.

Chapter 5:

Expectations, Values, and Priorities

BY NATURE, WE TEND TO SPEND VERY LITTLE TIME considering our beliefs about something. This is why college can be so eye-opening for people as they begin to challenge their long-held beliefs about almost everything. However, we all have assumptions about almost everything. I rarely have to explain to my clients that they sit on the couch and I sit on the chair in a therapy session, even if they've never been to counseling before.

Your assumptions about something create your expectations for it. This is important because you may often react to what you expect of your spouse without verifying those expectations in any way. You expect your spouse to react angrily so you don't tell them what they need to hear or approach them with a preemptive anger, even if they never get angry.

You expect your spouse not to meet your needs, so

you refuse to appear vulnerable or needy.

You may have an entire conversation in your head where the only response you've heard from your partner is what you assume or expect them to say *in your head* and then will respond to that conversation out loud. I cannot stress this point enough: often the conversation only occurred in your head.

Couples get stuck. They get stuck because they fail to offer a way to move forward, because they never stop to consider their expectations. Worse, they often act as if they have no expectations. They assume that if they can tell themselves they have no expectations, they will not be disappointed in people (the expectation being that people will always let them down). Because this expectation runs unchecked, they stumble through life unhappy and often malcontent.

If they are going to experience real change, they must look at their assumptions and their expectations. They must consider if the action they are about to take will get them the result they want to achieve.

Or will it *cost* them that result?

There are inherent dangers in this, of course. The most powerful lies are the ones we tell ourselves. The guy considering an affair is not going to honestly examine his expectations for how it will unfold. He's going to search for reasons to have the affair.

But if we can help him be honest about how it will probably turn out, he'll run a million miles in the other direction to avoid the affair.

To truly have the life you're looking for, you need to consider how your expectations are shaping your life and the choices you're making.

Let's move away from something as serious as an affair for a moment. The truth is that many couples get in trouble without ever having an affair or if there is an affair, the marriage dies long before the affair happens. Because people fail to consider what they should expect from their actions. Think about the man who stops talking to his wife because he's afraid of her reactions to almost everything or the woman who constantly criticizes her husband.

Both fail to consider the natural consequences of their actions. This often leads to actions that net the exact consequences they don't want.

The husband doesn't talk because he wants everything to be okay between him and his wife. The wife criticizes because she wants the job done right.

What neither considers is the fact that they are driving each other away. Eventually, the wife will find out whatever the husband is trying to avoid and it will be far worse than if he had just come clean with her in the first place. With each criticism, she drives a wedge between her and her husband that will take years to remove. With each lie or criticism, they are both slowly killing the relationship.

They think they're protecting it because they're failing to consider the natural expectations of what they're doing. If you asked the husband how many people successfully keep secrets from their spouse and have a good relationship, he would say next to zero. Which begs the question, why is he keeping things from his wife, hoping to have a good relationship?

If you asked the wife how motivated she was by constant criticism, she would suggest that her motivation from criticism is null. Yet, she acts the opposite of this as though constant criticisms will motivate her husband despite its complete lack of motivation for her.

And yet, they both will repeatedly engage in this behavior. They have a disconnection between their expectations (or belief system) and their actions. This messes up the whole system.

VALUES

Our values come from our belief system. Like a fully gestated baby, they are born there. Whatever you believe about your world begins the process of setting your values into motion. We make our priorities in our values box. But most of us have failed to differentiate our values; we have unexplored values or we live in direct contrast to our values.

Think about walking into your local grocery store. The person in front of you drops twenty dollars. What do you do? Most of us would return the money without hesitation. It's not that we don't like money, but we don't like money more than we like our integrity. Our integrity is worth more than twenty dollars. This is a "values decision."

UNDIFFERENTIATED VALUES

Choosing between our base values and our more altruistic values can be a difficult task. For instance, if you were angry with your spouse, you would not consider striking them. If you were cut off in traffic, you might get angry but you wouldn't run the person off the road. Why not? For some people, it's because they don't want to go to jail, but for many, it's because the idea of running someone off the road and putting their life in danger is wrong.

But what if you had to choose between feeling vulnerable and exposed, or feeling loved? What if the thing you want the most requires you to engage in the thing you fear the most?

We make our priorities in our values.

Think back to money. Money has no value in and of itself. But we can trade it for something that does have value to us. Think about the last thing you purchased. Whatever it cost you, it is safe for me to assume you liked it more than you liked the money in your pocket.

But then there is this thing called *buyer's regret*. This occurs when someone buys something and a little while later feels regret for the purchase. They failed to truly differentiate their own values. They acted on impulse.

This is a very good illustration for how people often sabotage their relationships.

UNEXPLORED VALUES

Kristina sat in my room on my couch and said to me, "It's not that I'm angry at him. I just don't feel anything toward him. I'm not angry, I'm not sad, I'm just *blah.*"

I told her that I didn't believe her.

I further explained that I thought she was greatly hurt by her husband and that her value of safety was overriding everything else in her life. This desire (value) of safety dictated that she try to be as numb as possible to avoid the pain of engaging with her husband.

This caused frustration in her life because she also had a value to be loved. Her problems came because these values were competing with each other and she had never developed the skill to differentiate between her values.

Without taking the time to differentiate between her values, she had no paradigm in how to order her decisions.

Think once again about money. As previously stated, money has no value. It cannot keep you warm, but you can trade it for heat. Money cannot keep you full, but you can trade it for food. Money's value is relative. One hundred dollars to a homeless person is a lot, but to a wealthy person, it is little.

The challenge is that we have to trade time for money (often), which is another value.

In order to make good life choices, we have to be able to explore our value and understand the difference each has for us.

In relationships, we often have values driving our actions that we don't really think much about.

For instance, our desire to feel emotionally safe may override our desire to feel intimate with our spouse. When this happens, we often do things and then later, we will state that we regret what we did. Sometimes, we will throw our hands in the air and lament that we don't know why we do what we do. Put simply: it's because our values took over without us giving them much thought.

They have become muscle memory. We no longer give them thought. They become the operating system by which we function. We have as much control over them as a skydiver has over gravity. They have given themselves over to its pull, just as we have given ourselves over to the pull of our emotions. In many ways, this isn't bad. Good habits are as hard to break as bad ones.

COMPETING OR CONTRADICTORY VALUES

Let's continue to explore the struggle between our desire to feel safe and our desire to feel intimate with our spouse. If our value to feel safe is number one on our value list, then we have a problem because it will directly interfere with our desire to be intimate.

Intimacy comes at a price. That price is often giving up the feeling of being safe so that we can be vulnerable. Vulnerability rarely feels safe and almost always brings pain. If safety (more specifically, perceived safety) is running the show, it will hinder our intimacy. But we may *want to want* intimacy more than we want safety. We may think we want intimacy more than we want safety. We may even tell ourselves that we want intimacy the most, but our actions work against it. This is what I referred to earlier as "wanting to want something."

This is often for two reasons. First, we fail to tell ourselves the truth. Whenever I cover this with people, they push back. "I'm a brutally honest person!" is one of the most common responses. I rarely bring this up before I have collected copious amounts of data to support my thesis, so I lay out my case. Begrudgingly, they often agree. I am fond of saying, "The most powerful lies are the ones we tell ourselves, because we often say them inside our head where there is no one to debate or dispute them." We do this because it's safe.

Second, we often confuse wanting to want something with actually wanting it. That is to say, we will often think we want something simply because we think we *should* want it or because we know it is better than what we are currently doing.

I see this often in business proposals. I know, this is a relationship book, but a business is just a relationship on a much bigger scale. Almost all of the principles you're reading in this book apply to business as well. People will have a dream. They will talk about their dream. They will tell others about their dream. They will doodle about their dream.

But…

They'll never actually attempt to execute the dream because the dream, when attempted, could fail. They choose the safety of talking about the dream over the potential joy of living the dream. Keeping the dream in your head is safer than actually trying to move it to your hands and feet. No one can criticize something that doesn't exist.

We do the same thing in relationships. Think about sex. One of the most common issues that couples fight about is sex. We all want to have sex, yet most of the research would suggest that initiating sex is one of the most terrifying things we do. Why? Because our partner could decline us. We often take that rejection as a personal rejection of us and the story in our head tells us that there is something wrong with us. This leads to fear, which leads to feeling unsafe, which leads to feeling anger, which often leads to actions that work against us being intimate. It should be noted that intimacy and sex are not the same thing. Sex is part of intimacy, but it is *not* intimacy.

Coming back to Kristina, we began to talk about her values. She told me she didn't respect her husband at all. I asked her if that was a value. She said something to the effect of, "Yes, I would like to respect my husband. I feel that would be important." In so doing, she perfectly articulated two key points. One, our values create values and impact each other. She didn't respect her husband because he didn't do things she thought he should. But the very idea of respecting him was a value. When these get mashed in her head, they become undifferentiated and unexplored values.

Ricardo, Kristina's husband, also had problems with his values. He wanted to have a great relationship. He also wanted to avoid conflict at all costs. Conflict was bad. Conflict had driven his parents apart and had caused him all sorts of grief as a child. This all-consuming value to avoid conflict ran Ricardo's decisions. Whenever Kristina would bring up something that hinted at conflict or unrest in her life, he would feel panic. Pure, unadulterated panic would take over. His heart rate would accelerate, his hands would get cold, and he would choose safety over intimacy. He would withdraw. He would drink to take away the edge.

This, in turn, would anger Kristina, and she would attempt to reach out through anger and feel rejected. So Ricardo would withdraw, and the vicious cycle would kick off.

It is important to recognize that they were both trying to reach out, and doing it in a way that ultimately proved destructive. One of the skills that they needed to develop was aligning their actions with their stated beliefs. Before they could do that, they had to align them with their stated values. But how many people can actually express their values? Don't believe me? Take out a sheet of paper and write out a family creed.

Seriously.

Go grab some paper and write the values by which your family will guide their lives. The first time I did it, I had almost one hundred ideas in a matter of minutes. Now, prioritize them. Can you find the top five? Now that you have the top five, can you order them? Now, if we were to put cameras in your life, would what we recorded show these top five values? Competing values come for all of us. Understanding this is key to real and lasting change (incidentally, that's probably another book).

At some point, everyone must simply choose their values that they want to live by and adjust their life actions accordingly. Which brings us to the next stage of how life functions.

Chapter 6:

Actions and Consequences

ACTIONS

OUR ACTIONS CAN SEEM LIKE THEIR OWN ENTITY floating around us as if we have no control over them. Sometimes, it's as if we do exactly the opposite of what we want to be doing. That's because we struggle to have actions that align with our stated or perceived values. I have a friend who has wanted to write a book for as long as I've known him, which is a little over three decades. To my knowledge and by his admission, he has never written one page of text. Why? Well, certainly, part of it is that he has competing values. He probably *wants to want* to write a book, but he also values the relative comfort of not being criticized. This value of comfort over creating causes a logjam in his actions.

Make no mistake: actions are where the proverbial

rubber hits the road. Actions are the measuring stick by which we judge what happens. At least for others, for ourselves, we tend to be more gracious. You've probably heard someone say that we tend to judge others by their actions and ourselves by our intentions. Reality dictates, though, that actions are required for almost anything. If you want your relationship to be better, you're going to have to do something that will lead to a better relationship. You must act.

Hope isn't a plan. It's a desire.

Want isn't an action. It's a thought.

Actions are what drive your life. Because of this, you must take total ownership of what you do. You rarely control what happens, but you 100 percent control how you respond to those happenings. When you give up that control, you become stuck in a quagmire of your own making.

So often I work with people who blame their problems on other people:

"My dad..."

"My mom..."

"My ex..."

To be sure, what happens to us has an effect on us, but if we are going to see true, lasting change in our life, we must take total ownership of the fact that we are 100 percent responsible for what happens. Does life happen to you or do you happen to life? That's what you need to decide. So many people passively watch their life float by and then try to overcome that passivity with intensity.

It rarely works. Action requires an expenditure of resources. They take something from us. We inherently know that actions have a cost and that means they have value. They explain to us and the world what we value. Look at your checking account statements and calendar, and you will see what you truly value. Your actions don't lie.

Sadly, we often lie to ourselves. We tell ourselves the comfortable truths about what we want to want, but our actions rarely back that up. Do an exercise with me. Take out a sheet of paper and write down what you believe are your life values. Now, let me ask you a question.

If I were to outfit your entire life with cameras and microphones—if you were to become your own reality show—what would the viewers conclude were your values? That's the power of actions: they shine light into the dark recesses of our own souls. They force us, if we allow them to do so, to look at our life and be honest about what we value and want. This can often be different from what we say we want or value.

Derek and Kim knew exactly what I was talking about when I met with them for the first time. Kim was crying. She was stuck in a repetitive and destructive cycle. She was caught in an emotional affair that cycled on again and off again. It had first come to light three months earlier, when the child's five-year-old son had asked Derek a question about a mutual friend, John.

Derek asked Kim about John and could tell something was off. Finally, she admitted that John had met them (Kim and their son) on a trip to her hometown in California. She promised it would stop. She swore that she would cut it off completely.

She did not.

She was caught again.

She swore she would stop.

She did not.

And the pattern recycled itself.

She kept saying to me, "This isn't what I want." At some point, Kim needed to admit that she was doing and getting *exactly* what she wanted. She may not have wanted the consequences from what she was doing, but she was doing what she wanted to do. No one was making her do it. She was choosing it. There was a payoff in it for her. A payoff that she probably instinctively knew would not last, but a payoff nonetheless.

If we are to experience change, we must first accept the brutal reality of our actions. We must admit and own the fact that we control our actions. Even if someone puts a gun to your head and gives you the choice of doing something horrendous or being shot, you still have the choice of how you respond. Healthy couples live in this principle because it is the only way they become healthy.

Understanding that I own my actions and that I am 100 percent responsible for them allows me to believe the same about my spouse. That means I can give her the freedom to be who she is and not try to control her. This is so important because it takes away our built-in excuse for bad behaviors. When we fail to take 100 percent responsibility for our actions, we will often utilize lame and poor excuses for bad actions.

"I wouldn't call her a bitch if she didn't..."
"I wouldn't be so controlling if he didn't..."
"Well, I don't mean to hit her, but she just disrespected me."
"I would have never cheated, but he was too involved at work."

These are excuses for poor behavior. Believe me, as a relationship therapist, I hear all sorts of these excuses. Sadly, as a husband, I've used them for my own poor behavior. Healthy couples refuse this seductively appealing trap. I have even heard people go so far as to say, "This isn't an excuse—it's a reason."

Sometimes, that's true. Most of the time, it's just an excuse.

Expect It to Be Hard

One of the most common responses I get from people when I work with them on how to get better at their relationships is, "What you're suggesting will be hard!" My answer is always a resounding yes! Yes, it will be hard! That's the nature of change and the nature of becoming better. It's hard. But often the destructive choices we make are equally as hard.

At least living in the consequences of them, which is the next and final box we need to consider.

CONSEQUENCES

Consequences naturally flow out of our actions. In the western world, we tend to think of consequences as only bad, but they are both good and bad. What day is payday? That day is a good consequence. You receive a paycheck as a positive or good consequence for going to work.

That's why you go to work, even on the days you don't want to go. You want that good consequence. But that truth illustrates something I want to be really clear about: you are 100 percent in control of your life. If you do not want to go to work tomorrow, you do not have to go. You can stay home.

The rub is that you have to be willing to live in the consequence of that choice. If you don't go to work, you don't get paid. Eventually, you'll lose your job. When you lose your job, you won't get money. When you don't get money, you won't be able to pay your bills. When you can't pay your bills, you'll lose possession of things. And the consequences continue.

This cavalcade of consequences happens in our relationships as well. It is what causes people to lose hope. They run into the place where they believe their consequences are a foregone conclusion. And to some extent, they are exactly that—at least until the next harvest can be planted, grown, and reaped.

Once you plant a crop, you get the harvest you planted. A couple of years ago, in my home state, we had an unusually warm spring. In March, the weather was so warm that flowers started to bloom. I have friends who are apple farmers. They were extremely worried because if the weather returned to normal, the plants would die and the crop would either fail or be far below expectations.

The weather *did* drop. Crops died. My friends were nervous. Sure, they had insurance, but that isn't as good as a healthy crop.

Farmers are a hearty lot. Especially the ones who are my friends.

In the face of losing their normal crop, they planted a different crop. They planted soybeans.

If the current crop of consequences that you are experiencing is not what you want to have, you can plant a new crop.

You just have to be willing to wait for it to mature.

So often people get stuck in reliving the same pattern again and again because they keep making the same choices. There is an old saying that if you want to get different results, you have to make different choices. This saying is true and important because people tend to think they need to change their consequences.

To some degree, people can't change their

consequences. It's as though they're trying to stop from getting wet by being outside in the rain. They need to do *something*. Actions change consequences. They are the only thing that changes consequences.

So if you're getting wet, you need to open an umbrella or come inside, get out of the rain. In the same way, if you don't like your life consequences, you need to change your actions. Of course, changing your actions may mean changing some values and a few tweaks to the belief system. We need to be able to recognize our consequences because they are what we live in.

The person who doesn't pay her bills will live in different consequences than the person who does pay her bills. But the difference between them isn't the consequences. Those are only a manifestation of the difference, which in reality is the actions. But more importantly, the difference is somewhere in their values (or belief system).

We cannot change one without going after the other. To change our actions, we need to look at our values and our belief system. Making changes there will eventually change our consequences.

This is how change works.

We tend to take our consequences and compare them to our expectations and assumptions. This is why some TV personalities have been successful in the past with questions like, "How'd that work for you?"

Because we all inherently know we can have a

tendency to do things that work against what we say we're looking to achieve. This causes us to feel stuck.

Think about work for a moment. You expect to get a paycheck for showing up every day. If you went to work on whatever day was payday and they told you, "Oh, we're sorry, but we don't actually have your money today. We'll have it in just a few days," how would you react? If you really liked your employer and your job, you might be okay with it once. If you're particularly gracious, you might even give the company a pass a second time. But it seems unlikely to me that anyone would stay in a job where that happened regularly.

We have an expectation that we will get paid for showing up. In the same way, imagine if you didn't show up. If you just didn't go in. At a couple places where I worked, it was called a "no-call, no-show." What's interesting to me was the different ways a no-call, no-show was handled by the each company.

At one place where I worked, if you were a no-call, no-show, you were fired immediately. It was rare for someone to be a no-call, no-show. At another place where I worked, management took more of a fluid response. Sometimes, people would be terminated; sometimes, they would get second chances.

And a third chance.

Sometimes, even a fourth or fifth chance.

Well, you get the idea. As you might imagine at the second place, people tended to just *not* show up a lot more than at the first place. The fact of the matter is that the employees were 100 percent in control of what they did at both places. They were able to choose completely whether or not they went to work. And in both places, the management was 100 percent in control of how they responded. The employer's response (action) became the consequences for the employee, which then created new actions from the employee, which were the consequences for the employer.

This is true in every relationship. Actions are cyclical and symbiotic. They feed each other. Our consequences are where we live. They are also the genesis for which our belief system is formed. This leads us to another important question: How do we develop our belief system? From where do our expectations come? So many people that I journey with feel stuck in a destructive cycle.

They feel stuck because they try to change their consequences without changing their actions. Worse, they often fail to consider what's driving their felt need to do the actions they simultaneously crave and hate. In the next chapter, I will examine our belief system in depth.

Chapter 7:

How Do We Form Our Belief System?

IFIND THE INTERNET TO BE AN AMAZING PLACE. There are people I follow on different social media platforms that I have never met in real life. I follow them all for different reasons. I follow some people because they posted something about how they changed. I'm obsessed with how people successfully change.

One such person is on a weight loss journey. I have been losing weight intentionally for almost two years so I am intrigued to follow others who are doing the same thing.

But this one person doesn't do things that actually help her lose weight. In fact, I am amazed at how many pictures are posted of her doing things that work directly against achieving her desired goal of losing weight.

There seems to be a cycle of a few weeks of parties and unhealthy choices, followed by a week or so of intensively restrictive choices. On and on the yo-yo of weight loss and gain spins for this person.

I believe this is because she is trying to make a change happen in her life without looking at her own belief system. The gained weight is just a consequence of her actions. Actions she states that she both loves and hates. If she wants to really see a change, she'll need to understand what her belief system is and how it was formed.

We form our belief system through the use of lenses. These lenses are not sequential. They are symbiotic. They live off of each other, and each person tends to put more emphasis on different lenses for his or her own reasons.

The four lenses we use are:
- Expectations
- Culture
- Internal dialogue
- Our experiences and interpretations of those experiences

Remember: these lenses do not operate in any particular order for everyone. We move them around throughout our life to meet our needs and the situation at hand. We tend to put more emphasis on one or the other for a variety of reasons. They are not linear; rather, they are more symbiotic.

Someone might put an emphasis on expectations, while another person might emphasize experiences and the interpretation of those experiences. Often, each person in a relationship will have a different order of the lenses. It is important that we understand how the lenses shape our life. Emotional security can grow when we can understand how our spouse's belief system is operating because it allows us deeper understanding and intimacy.

Let's look at each one.

EXPECTATIONS

I know it seems strange to say, but our expectations form our expectations. We all are prone to something called "confirmation bias." We tend to seek out facts that confirm our expectations and we tend to ignore those that contradict our hopes, which causes us to see what we expect to see. This is especially true when our emotions are running high or are in a dangerous and defeated spot. If we are going to process our emotions in a healthy way, we have to accept the fact that our expectations are a major lens for how we see what is happening. Consider my friend Steve.

He had a long day at work and was fairly certain that everything happening was the universe conspiring against him. He just couldn't catch a break. To make things worse, he and his wife Diane had a counseling appointment in the middle of the day. The counselor had promised that they were going to "really dig into the drinking issue next week." Steve was certain that the counselor was going to call him a drunk and side with his wife.

The session started fairly okay.

"Steve, do you think you have a drinking problem?" the counselor asked.

"No, to be honest, I don't."

"Why do you think your wife thinks that you do?"

"I have no idea—you'd need to ask her." He could feel his blood pressure rising. Here it was, she was going to side with his wife.

"But, I'm asking you," his counselor replied.

At this point, Steve was incensed. She had already asked the question and he had already answered it. He sat there fuming.

"Look, doc, I have no idea. I mean, I like to drink, but I pay all my bills, I show up to work on time, I don't drink and drive…" His words trailed off as he lost steam.

Steve never went back to that therapist. I know, because he told me about it weeks later. After he told me, he sat there looking at me expectantly. Waiting for me to weigh in. I looked at him, unsure what it was he wanted.

"You want me to tell you what I think of her approach?" I asked.

"Well, yeah, you are a counselor and all."

"Okay, can I ask you a question first?"

He looked at me puzzled as if he were wondering what question I could possibly ask him. "Sure, I suppose, go ahead."

"Well, what were you hoping she would do?"

"What do you mean?" he asked.

I looked at him directly and asked, "Do you agree that the alcohol is a problem between you and Diane?"

"Absolutely" was his unequivocal reply.

"And you feel like it needed to be addressed?"

"Of course. Diane needs to get off my back. The last thing I need is someone else berating me about my drinking."

"But how did she berate you? She just asked you why you thought Diane had a problem with how much you drink. It actually seems like a reasonable line of questioning to me. It seems to me that you had expected her to be on Diane's side so it didn't matter what she asked or how she asked it—you were already primed to be on the defensive. Your expectations created your lens that you saw her actions through."

For a moment, I thought he was going to accuse me of being on the therapist's side. Instead, he just looked at me and said, "Oh, man! I do that all the time. It's something Diane complains about nonstop."

I encouraged him to consider what change would look like and to consider going back to the therapist and re-engaging the process.

CULTURE

Our culture forms us in two ways. There is the culture we come from and the culture that we hope to aspire to become. The culture we come from is the one we all tend to understand. We all seem to innately understand that we do certain things because that is how they were done in the household in which we grew up. There are the cute and fun aspects of our culture from our youth. How you decorate the house for Christmas, the fact that you eat pie on your birthday instead of cake, or the little sayings you have that mean something to you and your loved ones but not the same thing to everyone else.

Then, of course, there are those other culture makers. If you had a parent who was constantly assuming that everyone was talking down to them or insulting them, you or one of your siblings probably have similar actions. In fact, almost everything that is from your past culture is somehow rooted in your upbringing. Maybe you came from a culture that told you implicitly or explicitly that women are not to have a voice, that disagreeing with their husband is akin to killing a small liter of kittens with her bare hands. If, perhaps, you came from this culture, you might be tempted to always just admit you were wrong and never question your husband. You might apologize even if you think you did not do anything wrong. Eventually, you might become resentful of your husband because you have lived in the way that your culture dictates. Every time you and he argue, you hear your mother's voice like a cackling crow sending shivers of distress down your spine.

The culture you come from shapes your experiences, like a gardener shapes a plot of land. Some gardeners shape land in such a way as to create an inviting atmosphere while others are not interested in creating a space for others to visit. And yet, others neglect their duties of gardening and ignore their plot of land. This plot becomes overrun with weeds of sorrow and burrs of regret. These gardens are all shaped by the gardener and those shapes mold the experience of those who enter. These experiences then shape future expectations for the same experience.

JERRY AND LUCY

Jerry ground his teeth inside his suddenly dry mouth. He prepared himself to ask Lucy why she had taken a certain route. They were both on their way to the beach, which was about twenty miles from their house. As he looked up from his book, he noticed they were going a way he didn't expect to go. He was afraid to say anything because they had been in a continuous cycle of fighting. He was expecting a fight with her. This expectation caused his heart rate to increase. He felt his palms go sweaty. His temples started to throb.

His response of fight, flight, or freeze began to kick in. His body was preparing for war.

Logically, he had no current reason for this expectation. His wife looked perfectly calm sitting behind the wheel. She had been in a good mood all morning and they had gotten along rather well. Yet, he was certain they would fight, no matter how carefully he chose his words. This expectation put Lucy at a severe disadvantage. To compound this issue, she had no idea how he was feeling. She would have agreed with him about the morning and how the day had gone. She also would have agreed that they had been in a bad patch, but she figured it was more of a temporary rough patch than a permanent place to be.

Jerry took a deep breath and began to speak his carefully chosen words…

Experiences and Interpretations of Those Experiences

Have you ever wondered why two couples can have almost the same fight with totally different results? Why can one couple go through the same stress and be more comfortable with each other, more in love, and have a better overall relationship? The other couple becomes less comfortable with each other and more distrustful of each other, and has a worse relationship from nearly the same conflict. The difference isn't because of the experiences, but because of the interpretation of the experience.

Why is the color blue, blue? Typically, when I ask people this question, they tell me because their brain processes it as blue. Which only begs another question: Why does their brain interpret it as blue and not green?

96

Is it not because we have decided that blue will be blue and green will be green? It's not the blue or the green that has declared itself to be blue or green; we have agreed that our interpretation of our experience will dictate those colors.

It's the same way in relationships. Our interpretations of our experiences arc what gives them meaning and forms our expectations for the next time we encounter them.

A couple can have a conflict and walk away from it with minimal damage if they have an expectation that the other person is seeking what's best for the relationship and the couple. This belief comes, at least in part, from the interpretation of past experiences.

This interpretation is one of the ways we compare our consequences to our expectations. We interpret the value and meaning of something that happened. This interpretation both gives past experiences meaning and forms our expectations for future incidents. If their past experiences of engaging in conflict with their partner was damaging and painful, they will come to expect the future experiences to be painful and damaging. Because of this expectation, they will often disengage.

This is the wizardry of marriage counseling: helping couples to come to the place where they believe that engaging is not only important but also necessary and productive for healthy relationships.

INTERNAL DIALOGUE

Everything in our life is driven by what is being said inside our heads. We all have that internal voice that runs almost nonstop. In many ways, it is a powerful tool that helps us throughout the day. That internal voice helps to shape our belief system. It helps us form our expectations about what might happen, about what *should happen.* This creates our assumptions as well.

In many driver safety courses, part of the curriculum will often focus on planning by telling yourself a story about what could happen. I remember when I took a safety class for my motorcycle license, and I was told to always look for a way out if someone in front of me did something I didn't expect them to do. The best way I know to do this is to utilize my internal dialogue.

When I was a high school sports coach, I often told my athletes to utilize their internal dialogue to imagine the upcoming game. They should hear the story about what they would do and what their opponent would do. How would the game go? What would the jerseys look like? How would the officiating go? This is utilization of the internal dialogue to prepare for good things to happen.

I once read a book that talked about how an Olympic swimmer had trained using his internal dialogue to prepare for everything from his goggles filling with water to someone illegally coming into his lane. One time, his goggles did break and he was prepared because he had used his internal dialogue to visualize what it would look and feel like if they broke. Furthermore, he used the same technique to visualize what he would do when it happened. He used his words to create pictures of success in his head. Our brain cannot tell the difference between our visualization and our real-life experiences.

Of course, this also works in reverse. You could play out an entire conversation in your head before you ever actually engage in that conversation. This internal dialogue can tell you all sorts of things that are negative as well.

I often meet people who tell me they don't engage potential change because of the voice inside their head telling them why it will fail. This internal dialogue creates an expectation (belief system) of failure. In this expectation, inaction is born.

Chapter 8:

Conflict Is Your Best Friend

STORYTELLERS LOVE CONFLICT. SERIOUSLY. THINK about our modern-day bards—they all tell tales of high conflict. This conflict gives the hero or heroine in the story purpose and meaning. It challenges the heroine to overcome. The hero chases down monsters and faces certain destruction. The consumer of these stories will often sit with rapt attention as the conflict unfolds.

Many times, the consumer will relate to the heroine in some way and will seek to tell a similarly great story with their own life. They typically have a problem, though. The great story they want to tell will require them to engage in conflict.

They hate conflict. The run from it as though it were a plague promising the most violent death. They believe conflict is the problem.

Well, of course, the problem isn't actually *conflict*.

It's their *belief* about conflict. That belief drives our assumptions about conflict and those assumptions ultimately drive our actions regarding conflict.

To help me illustrate my point, do me a favor. Take out a piece of paper. Any size will do, but a notebook size is ideal for this exercise.

Draw a circle in the middle of it.

Write the words "Circle of Conflict" in the middle of that circle. Now populate the rest of the page with everything you do in your normal life. If it's part of your life, put it on the sheet. Your sheet should look like the drawing below except where mine reads "hobbies," yours might list the actual hobbies.

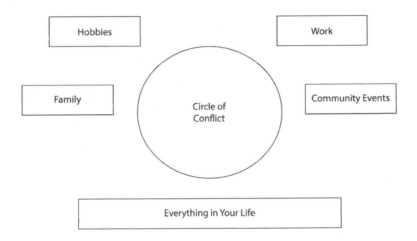

Now let me ask you a question: What if I told you that the only way to get to the healthy, vibrant relationship you want is to go through that circle? Moreover, you have to go in that circle and stay there until you can solve the conflicts in your life.

Almost everyone I meet has an assumption that that circle is the most dangerous place in the world for them to spend time. They avoid the circle of conflict as though death itself inhabits it. It is impossible to live our life outside the circle. We cannot spend our entire life avoiding conflict.

This is the root of passive-aggressive behavior.

Go back to your paper. Draw a line running around the circle that darts in and out of the circle. This is how almost everyone I come across handles conflict. They get in long enough to feel a little better and then get out. This is destructive to healthy, happy, and thriving relationships because it tells the other person we are more concerned about our own comfort than we are about the well-being of the relationship or them.

It makes us untrustworthy to the other person. The best-case scenario is that we have a stockpile of other behaviors to cause the person to believe we are trustworthy. This stockpile may be destroyed when we engage conflict with the other person because we will probably reveal our own deceit. This duplicity will cause pain in the other person.

In order to have healthy relationships, we must be willing to do the following three things:

1. Engage conflict in a healthy manner.
2. Stay engaged in conflict long enough to resolve the issue.
3. Find a way to exit the circle of conflict in a

manner that reflects the fact that we resolved the issue and leave the issue there. We must find a healthy way to disengage.

What If I Could Show You a New Way?

Which brings me to my favorite question to ask couples: What if I could show you a way to go through conflict and come out the other side with a stronger relationship? Would you be interested? Okay, that's two questions, but think about that possibility for a moment. It can literally be life-changing.

We have to create a culture in our families and communities that comes to appreciate conflict for the beautiful opportunity that it is. Yes, you read that correctly: I believe that conflict is a beautiful opportunity. Conflict lets us know we are being shaped by those we are in a relationship with. We are being changed.

Conflict is an opportunity to grow. More importantly, it's an opportunity to show those we love that we care about them more than we care about our own comfort or more accurately, our discomfort. We are saying, "I care more about our relationship than I do about seeking perceived safety. I want our relationship to grow and be deeper so I'm going to stay involved in a way that is not destructive and seek to deepen our relationship."

This is vital for relationships to be healthy. Conflict

allows relationships to grow and to be strengthened through the process. What's worse is that when conflict is avoided, it's often avoided in dangerous and unhealthy ways.

We try to suppress our conflict by pretending it doesn't exist and stuffing our feelings deep down inside of us. Like a poison, it spreads through our bodies, infecting us internally before eventually destroying us externally. We must learn how to handle conflict, and we must enter the circle of conflict long enough to solve the conflict.

Sometimes, we don't try to suppress the conflict. Sometimes, we try to avoid conflict by razing the ground it stands on. We attempt to avoid conflict by scaring it. We falsely believe we can scare conflict by scaring the people with whom we have the conflict. We do this by yelling at those people or using sarcasm. We attempt to hurt them because we believe that will give us safety. We're wrong, but we do it again and again.

Like a scratched LP, we return to the same tired and skewed tune because we view conflict as threatening and lack the emotional intelligence to differentiate between those we love and conflict. It is this ability that we must cultivate and develop.

At least part of my mission is to show you that conflict is good. Conflict is necessary to create healthy relationships. Society has become so conflict adverse that we are killing relationships with the very means with which we are trying to protect them.

Conflict has several benefits:

1. Conflict tells the other person that you love them more than you love your own comfort. Everyone knows we hate conflict. Your partner knows how much you hate it (even if you're running around blowing people up and loving the drama, which is another day). By engaging properly in conflict, we tell our partner we love them more than we love our own security. You are telling your spouse you love them and will engage in difficult things to grow that love.

2. Conflict allows your relationship to grow by moving both parties into deeper water. So often, we want a deep relationship, but we're afraid to wade into the deep waters of our emotions to experience it. This creates a shallow that seems safe but in reality is truly dangerous. You simply cannot have a deep relationship that never leaves the shallow waters of total agreement. Whenever I do premarital counseling, I will ask the couple to tell me about their last two fights. To be certain, I get nervous if they tell me that they fight all day, every day. I get more nervous if they tell me that they never fight. I wonder how deep their relationship can truly be if they've never pushed off shore and truly plumbed the depths of their emotions.

3. Conflict helps each person to become a better version of themselves. Conflict shapes you. It changes who you are and who you are becoming, if you allow it to do so. The difficult reality is that even if you don't want it to change you, it still will. Avoiding conflict will just change you into someone you don't want to become. The same result will happen if you simply engage in conflict but refuse to process it. Processing is accepting what happened and the feelings that were experienced. Processing starts with the experiences and feelings and ends with a discussion about what kind of person you want to be and how you want to react to those experiences and feelings.

4. Conflict teaches us to differentiate our emotions. One of the best abilities that everyone can foster is to differentiate between emotions. This is often very difficult because we are uncomfortable dealing with any emotions, including our own. Because of this discomfort, we often run to the delusional safety of the emotions that we use the most. One of the most common emotions we feel in a relationship is fear (vulnerability is probably more accurate), but we tend not to know how to deal with fear so we deal with it by being angry—because anger is what we are used to using. Like a dog that sits on your lap sharing its heat and then suddenly gets up. When your dog leaves, you shiver. When your anger leaves, it too often leaves you with a shiver. That shiver scares you and you react by fueling more anger.

5. Conflict fosters teamwork. There is no better skill for a couple to develop than teamwork. Teamwork is what allows them to handle the difficulties of marriage and parenthood. Indeed, teamwork helps them to navigate the difficulties of life—and life is hard.

Marriage and family are about connection. Teamwork is connection.

6. Conflict develops our self-control. We all have a built-in response to conflict. For many people, that response is destructive to the health of their relationships. Engaging in conflict affords each of us the opportunity to develop our use of those responses. That is the epitome of self-control.

7. Conflict creates a repository of memories that affirms to us that our relationship is secure. One of the key signs of a healthy couple is the litany of memories they have regarding conflicts that have been resolved. Your willingness to engage in conflict with your loved one is, in a very real sense, exposure therapy.

I have a friend who loves spending time in nature. He recently bought a portable hunting stand for his photography. There was one major problem: he's extremely afraid of heights. He went up just a few feet and began to have a panic attack. He talked himself down but was ready to quit the use of the stand. A friend encouraged him to keep it and go up again. The next time, he went up a few more feet and just sat there. Eventually, he was able to use the stand as it was intended. What he did to himself was an example of *exposure therapy*. He allowed his body to experience that which it feared and mentally catalogued the results. As a result, he was creating a cache of memories that told his body and emotions that going up that tree was safe. This is what we do when we engage our fear of conflict.

There's a Native-American saying: "The wolf in your head is often louder than the wolf in the field." I have no idea if that saying is accurately ascribed, but I will say I have found truth in those words both personally and professionally.

8. Conflict creates emotional security. Ultimately, conflict creates emotional security and that is our goal! We cannot have a healthy and vibrant relationship without having gone through conflict. It is impossible. By engaging in the conflict and staying engaged long enough to solve the problem, we create rich soil for emotional security to take root and grow.

If you are both willing to engage in conflict without blowing each other up and if you are both willing to sit in the discomfort of conflict and fear of anger that comes with every relationship without demanding false safety by using hurtful words, you can build your own memory list of danger avoided by being together. This is the essence of emotional security.

Handling conflict is like any other skill we need. It takes time to learn. It takes practice. Rarely do I find couples willing to practice. Practice requires handling conflict with intentionality. Practice requires forcing ourselves to be proactive until the action we want becomes our reaction.

If you don't practice these tools to improve your relationship, they will do nothing for you. They will simply take up space.

Chapter 9:

Who or What Is Driving Your Bus?

Have you ever wondered why some couples can joke and laugh and no one seems to be offended, while at the same time another couple will go into a tailspin that will threaten to crash their marriage for weeks over the same joke?

I once had a couple ask me this very question. The husband and I were sitting at one of my favorite places, a coffee shop. At the time, I was not working as a counselor, but even then, I was doing a lot of counseling and very interested in relationships. My friend stated to me point-blank, "I don't understand why I can't joke with my wife. Other guys seem to be able to do it and it's no big deal. It frustrates the heck out of me."

I have to admit, I have found his assessment to be true. My wife and I have often marveled at the things some of our friends will fight over. We have encountered many couples who had something happen that caused a fight while we had laughed at a similar situation. One time, a couple told us about a fight they had over how well one of them drove. My wife and I constantly joke about the other's driving.

What is the difference? The answer is probably long and nuanced, but I think it can be summed up to a rather simple question. Do you feel safe? Does your spouse feel safe with you? What drives your relationship?

The question becomes: What is driving your bus? By and large, we have two operational drivers: fear and love. When we operate out of fear, we will often do destructive and dangerous things. Our relationships will suffer because all relationships by their very nature require risk. Risk is counterproductive to living in fear. Ask yourself these four questions:

1. What am I most afraid of in my relationship?
2. What is my spouse most afraid of in our relationship?
3. What do I want most out of my relationship with my spouse?
4. What does my spouse want the most out of our relationship?

These four questions encompass the idea of fear or love driving the bus, which is your relationship.

What happens when fear drives the bus? What happens when the thing driving the bus is taking us to the exact opposite place we want to go? It seems obvious: we need to change drivers.

We all know that love isn't enough for relationships

to actually work and flourish. A friend of mine said that "trust and respect are the pillars that hold love up in every relationship." Every relationship either works off of love, trust, and respect or guilt, shame, and fear. When the narrative of the relationship between two people revolves around love, trust, and respect, the narrative builds emotional security. It can endure anything.

When the relationship revolves around guilt, shame, and fear, it will almost always go badly. Guilt, shame, and fear are insidiously dangerous because they give us a temporary feeling of control but ultimately rob us of any lasting direction. No matter the topic, no matter the issue, guilt, shame, and fear will always destroy. It will always rob us of everything.

WHEN FEAR DRIVES THE BUS

Think about people who might be afraid of conflict. How would this play out in a relationship? Will acting out of fear of conflict actually improve the relationship or will it hurt and ultimately destroy the relationship? In the beginning, the relationship will have a small and inaccurate feeling of control. Of course, the feelings creating the conflict are not going to go away. The couple is still going to feel frustration and anger. They are still going to feel the stress of possibly not being connected. When these feelings come, they aren't going to engage in them because that would lead to conflict, which is what they are avoiding because of fear. So they avoid the idea of actually disagreeing and getting into a conflict.

At first, this feels wonderful. Well, that's not true. It feels better than the monster that fear has made out of conflict. This is what fear does: it creates monsters. It doesn't usually exist in the moment, but typically looks forward to *what could happen.* In this scenario, it looks forward to what the conflict will become. It looks forward to all the things the other person is going to say. It looks toward all the hurt that will come from actually engaging in conflict. It doesn't see any good that could come from it, but it does see all the potential problems that could come from being in conflict. So by avoiding one monster (conflict), we create another, even more sinister monster (detachment).

Overtime, this monster grows. It becomes something of mythical proportions. It becomes insurmountable. The relationship must die in the face of this all-consuming monster. The only way for the relationship to survive is to avoid the conflict at all costs. Of course, this move to protect the relationship actually begins to destroy the relationship because conflict that goes unprocessed becomes like a poison. It infects and destroys everything it touches.

What if a person is afraid they might do something that will cause their spouse to leave? Now, I'm not talking about things like having an affair or an addiction. I'm talking about *anything* that could happen. They're afraid if they pick the wrong restaurant or if they express their frustration about something in the wrong way, it will cause their spouse to leave. What do they do? They become spineless. They roll over and do nothing. I cannot tell you how many times I have seen a couple enter this phase and one person is scared to death to actually try anything, thinking this lack of action will help the spouse to realize how much they are loved.

Instead, it drives them further away.

GUILT

Guilt and shame run together like best friends holding hands through a field of heather. What happens when the relationship becomes guilt-based? Someone does something they know will not be appreciated by the other partner. This legitimate guilt creates fear. Maybe someone has an emotional affair. They come clean, but there is no real processing of the pain and betrayal. Instead, the cheater works hard to make sure that the "even" is put in the past, and the one who is cheated on brings up the pain and betrayal as often as possible because they want to make sure the other person knows how much they've been hurt. They falsely believe that somehow their pain will be lessened if the other person feels some of it.

This can be known as guilt-tripping. The person who did the cheating begins to think that they will be paying for their transgression for the rest of their life, which seems like a punishment that is not commiserate with the severity of their crime. When a fight happens, the "event" comes up again and again. It is used as a whip to keep them in line.

Meanwhile, the person who was cheated on is terrified (fear) that they could be hurt again so they want to leverage the other person's guilt to ensure they will not be hurt again. They use the person's guilt by inducing shame. Often, this is not even a conscious thought process. It simply happens, like muscle memory. Both people are desperate for control, for the feeling of being safe. This desire causes them to spiral through guilt, shame, and fear attacking each other. This spiral tears their relationship apart.

Like passengers on a bus, they and their relationship go wherever the bus driver takes them. Often, these drivers lead them straight to emotional insecurity and divorce. Under the crushing weight of guilt, shame, and fear, they find themselves in a constant cycle of emotional pain and furious verbal fights that leave them drained, hurt, and resentful.

SHAME

When we feel insecure or are afraid that something in our narrative is going to cause us pain, we may try to avoid that pain by shaming someone into line. I see parents do this the most with their children. They use phrases that attempt to connect with their child's shame and use that to motivate them into obedience.

It usually works for the short-term. They say phrases like: "After all I do for you..." or "What's wrong with you?"

GUILT, SHAME, AND FEAR HAVING POSITIVE EFFECTS

There is a problem that is inherent in this part of the conversation. In proper doses, these emotions can be somewhat beneficial.

Often, I will talk about the issue of guilt, shame, and fear having some positive effects for relationships. I don't want to spend a lot of time on this topic, but yes, I believe that these emotions can be beneficial. That is to say, there are things that should cause me to feel guilt or shame. If I yell at my wife or call her names, I should feel guilt and shame. It should spur me on to make changes. Guilt, shame, and fear are not the problem per se, but using them as possessive control is the problem. Building a relationship with them as the base is the problem.

Fear can be beneficial. The fear of death can cause us not to do things we should probably avoid. Fear can add a few ounces of effort in a life-threatening situation. Fear of negative consequences can keep us from doing certain things we might be tempted to do over the course of our life. These negative emotions can be helpful in small doses. They cannot and should

117

not be used for long-term control. At some point, we must move from action-based on negatives to action-based on positives (i.e., actions based on doing the right thing). Relationships that are based on guilt, shame, or fear always break down. They almost always look good for a short time and then it all starts to fall apart. Simply put: we are not made to live in that type of environment.

Maybe you know exactly what I mean. Maybe you're living with guilt, shame, and fear as constant companions of your relationship. Maybe you and your spouse constantly fight. I have good news. You don't have to be on a bus driven by guilt, shame, and fear. You don't have to be caught in a spiral of anger, verbal violence, and withdrawal. You can be on a bus driven by love, trust, and respect. What would that look like?

When a relationship is being driven by love, trust, and respect, things can go wrong. Tempers can flare, but it doesn't lead to a vicious fight. Space is created for each partner to have bad days, but it doesn't become personal. Each person has the opportunity to truly bare his or her soul and truly live in emotional security.

LOVE

Someone once famously asked, "What is love?" What does a relationship look like that has love as a pillar? I think for most people, love is like a mythical pot of gold. It sounds nice in theory, but when it actually comes down to putting love into action, the idea is terrifying. What does it mean to love someone else? What does it mean to love another person unconditionally? We all want to be loved unconditionally, but I think even more accurately, we all want to be a person who loves someone else unconditionally.

Over the years, I've asked many people to define love for me. I've heard almost as many different answers as I have met different people. What is love? How does it work in a relationship? Everyone pays lip service to the idea that love is forever, but most people don't know how to do that in our messy, broken world. Think about your vows. Who says, "I promise to love you forever, until you screw up completely"? No one.

Added to our own angst about the idea of love is our experiences. Too many have felt the sting of abandonment and rejection. They have watched people walk away. Despite original promises of unending love and everlasting commitment, loss and abandonment have entered the narrative. The pain is so much that we almost develop a PTSD response to it, where any time the possibility of being hurt enters the script, it is abandoned for the illusion of safety and security.

But love is about risk. I once heard someone say, "To love someone is to invite pain."

Without risk, we cannot love. Love is inherently a risk. That's part of what makes it so valuable. We cannot give love without giving ourselves away. Love is so complex and so beautiful that it requires us to paint pictures of it with metaphors and word pictures so we can define it. I believe love is saying, "I will give the best of me for the best of you regardless of what you do."

Isn't that terrifying?

Isn't that hope-filling?

When love is a pillar of a relationship, disagreements are no longer scary—they are an opportunity to grow in love. They are a gateway to deeper understanding and affection. They are the path to plumbing the depths of your partner's soul for the hidden gems that make them, them! Conflict becomes a means to grow our relationship because it becomes the mechanism by which you and I become *we*.

In a relationship, this means you can be really angry with each other and not have to worry about the end of your relationship nearing. It means you can be extremely hurt and learn to forgive. It means that no matter what happens, the two of you can work it out together.

That's the key word though, *together*. For love to truly be a pillar of a relationship, it has to be built into the relationship by both people. If one person is constantly building into the relationship by giving of herself and the other person is not building into the relationship but is attacking the relationship with selfishness, then it will eventually crumble and fall apart. Relationships are not built by one person, but two. We cannot force someone else to love us. We can only love them and offer ourselves to them.

When love is truly a pillar of the relationship, words of affirmation are a regular part of the story. Positive events that occur—no matter how small—are magnified and ruminated upon. Moments of stress can be tolerated because they are not the normal pattern of life. Even intense moments of anger can be endured because the anger is about the person's actions, not the person.

TRUST

When a relationship has trust as a pillar, it withstands the slower seasons of marriage. What happens when trust is the driver of a relationship? Before I answer that, let me ask you a question. Take a few moments to answer and see if you can remember a few real-life instances that back up your answer. When something is said in your relationship and it can be taken either in a good or bad way, how is it taken? Relationships that have trust as a pillar tend to be far higher on the taken in the best possible way.

Trust is assuming that the other person is doing the best possible thing for the relationship and each other. Mistakes happen and are more easily processed because of the trust factor. Mistakes, fights, and missteps will always be a part of every relationship's narrative, but trust helps each person navigate those problems.

No one expects perfection, but when a lack of trust enters the relationship, fear begins to run rampant in the relationship.

Trust is the antidote to the relationship poison that is fear.

Trust is built one step at a time between two people.

But trust is not earned. I know, I know. You just told me I'm wrong as you read those words. You may even be considering just walking away and ranting. Go ahead, I'll wait.

Trust is *given*.

There is always something more we can make the person do to "earn" our trust. There is always something more we can hold over them. Ultimately, we have to decide to give trust or to withhold it.

I have to give my wife trust, and she has to give me trust.

Or there is no trust.

The person who has been hurt (often it's both) waits until they feel like the other person has earned their trust. What they typically mean is that they are waiting for the other person to do something that is going to make their fear of being hurt go away.

But it will not. Fear usually diminishes when it is pushed down.

In order for trust to *be* trust, it has to be given with the possibility that it will fail. It has to scare the person who is giving it. If it doesn't bring a little fear, it's not trust.

Eventually, of course, trust becomes part of the relationship to the degree that there really is no fear.

This is the relational equity aspect that I talked about earlier. As trust builds and the relational equity grows, the trust becomes a bigger influence or driver in the relationship.

When this happens, love and respect can grow like roots for a healthy relationship.

RESPECT

Respect is an interesting concept in our language. Especially today, people think that respect equals agreeing with everything that a person says or does. Nothing could be further from the truth.

Respect is recognizing the other person's rights to make any decision they wish to make and your ability to choose how to respond. Respect is understanding that you can disagree with someone without shaming them or using invectives.

Respect is an individual interaction that will look differently for each couple. This is why it is so important for each couple to talk about what respect will look like in their relationship.

Respect recognizes that one person cannot control another person. Respect seeks to be kind and compassionate while engaging in the difficult emotions. Respect honors the differences between people while drawing appropriate boundaries.

Ultimately, respect is about holding the truth that all humans have worth. Humanity is as messy as a kitchen after a two-year-old's birthday party. We are often tempted to do what I call "Disneyfication" of life. I admit, I enjoy Disney movies. I like movies where the good guys are clearly good and the bad guys are clearly bad. I like nice, neat lines where the bad guys are all bad, with no redeeming good in them unless we find it in the last minutes of the movie before we cut to the somber music and the closing credits.

But in real life—let's just admit that phrase has to be used too often today when talking about relationships—the line between good and bad is so much more complicated. There was an ancient writer who once wrote about how much he disliked himself. He struggled because he found that he rarely did the things he wanted to do and he often found himself doing things he didn't want to do. To make matters worse, he felt like the things he didn't want to do, he would constantly fall back into doing. He actually pined for someone to rescue him from his wretched life. Many of my clients have similar thoughts.

That is real life.

People we love are rarely all good or all bad. They do things that are hurtful, sometimes on purpose. Respect says that no matter what they do, we can choose our words wisely. We do not have to repay meanness for meanness. We can respect their humanity.

Respect means that we regard the other person as a whole, complicated person. Furthermore, it means that no matter what they do, we act in an appropriate manner.

Chapter 10:

It's the Story We Are Telling

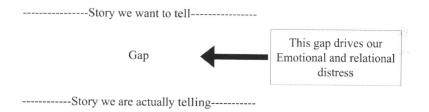

THERE'S ALWAYS A DIFFERENCE BETWEEN THE STORY we want to tell and the story we are living. No matter how much you like your job, there are things about it you *don't* like. You accept this, and you manage it as life moves on. For instance, I love what I do. Every day, I encounter new situations and problems that need to be solved regularly. The pace matches my personality and as an added bonus, I get the opportunity to help people.

I also like riding my motorcycle. I live in West Michigan so there are about four days a year when I can ride with the sunshine on my face. There is an inherent problem, though. Sometimes, on those sunny days, I have to work even if I do not want to go to work.

Sometimes, as part of that job, I have to do paperwork. I hate doing paperwork. The gap between my desire to ride my motorcycle and having to go to work or the gap between my love of my job and my distaste for paperwork must be tolerated if I am going to achieve anything worthwhile in life. In order for you to manage your life, you have to accept these gaps as well.

We come with a built-in tolerance for the gap. However, sometimes that gap grows bigger than we are prepared for it to grow. The difference between what we want to be telling and the story we are telling becomes too great.

In that moment, we usually make a bad decision. Our choices become maladaptive ones. We make these bad choices because we think they will make the gap smaller but in reality, our choices make the gap larger.

The best way to illustrate this is for parents. Sometimes, I do parenting conferences and I will ask how many parents think that yelling is the best way to motivate their children.

Almost always, no hands go up.

Then I ask how many yelled at their children within an hour of coming to the conference. Typically, half the hands in the room will go up. By the time I get to twenty-four hours before, almost all of the hands in the room are up.

This is a perfect example of living in a way that is incongruent with how we say we want to live (or the story we want to tell) because we feel threatened in some way.

This happens in relationships often. Especially the ones that are caught in a negative narrative. You are living your life and bump into conflict and you feel threatened.

So you react poorly.

This creates a negative narrative. That negative narrative causes you more stress. Suddenly, you're telling a story you don't want to be telling, but you're not sure how to get out of it.

This will destroy your hope.

Hope destroyed is a relationship destroyed.

Thoughts lead to feelings, which lead to emotions. It is usually out of these emotions that we react to many situations. How many Facebook conversations have you had that spun out of control because one person had an emotional reaction to what another person was saying? We believe we can't change what we are thinking.

But we can. First, we have to understand where that emotional reaction is coming from inside of us.

We are all telling a story with our life. When you think of yourself, you see yourself in some sort of role in the greater story of your life.

Maybe you feel like you're a victim, or maybe you feel like you are a cynic or a prosecutor. Maybe you believe you're the hero. I have met many people who are happy with the story they are telling in their life. I have also met many people who are not happy with the story they are telling. This creates distress in their emotional life, which often presents emotional distress in their physical life.

The greatest relief for this is to become really great listeners. A great listener will hear his partner's words but will ponder the depth of the emotional meaning behind those words.

As he does this, he will find that he can invite his wife into a different story, a better story.

Of course, this means we have to explore some deep and often disturbing ideas. What is it that makes a great story? What would be a great story for your life? What do you want to be known for? When your life ends, how you will measure it? As I stated earlier, I ask that often to people and the most common answer is, "I don't know."

Have you ever seen someone get angry when they didn't know the answer to a question about something deep in life? Have you ever been angry when someone has asked you if your life was a great story? Why?

I wonder if it isn't because people tend to believe that not knowing the answer is confirmation that they are failing or screwing up.

This belief of screwing up drives them to fear, which produces anger.

Good communication attempts to get to these emotions and works at creating hope in our partner that there is a great story to tell. I imagine that some day this idea should get its own book.

THREE CORE QUESTIONS

We all have three core questions that we strive to answer every day. They come from deep inside us. They all lead to the biggest question of all: "Am I loved?" We must have these questions answered in order to have the relationships we want. Our three core questions are:

1. Am I being heard?
2. Am I being valued?
3. Am I safe to share with my partner emotionally?

Problems come because we all have people who have hurt us, because they have answered these core questions in the negative. They have not listened to us and they have proven that we were not safe with them, nor were we valued by them. Then new people come into our life and they want us to trust them. They want us to love them. They want us to believe that they love us. But why should we trust them? Why should we believe them when the people who have come before them have hurt us in ways that we have not even begun to fathom yet?

Because of past hurts, we either pull away, or more likely, we learn to function by not allowing anyone to get too deep. As a society, we are "deep" phobic. Think about most of your interactions with people. How does the average one go? Is it something where you say, "Hi, how are you?" to someone and when they respond by unloading their struggles, you are left wondering what happened? All you did was say hi. We expect nothing more than "fine" when we greet someone.

Now, recall a time when you were on the other side of that. Recall a time when you were the one who felt like you needed to unload and you could not. Not being heard is one of the most frustrating things we will endure during our time here on earth.

Jane knew exactly what I meant when she heard me talk about the need to feel heard. Tears flowed freely as she talked about her relationship with Robert.

"He's so busy all the time. I don't want to sound like a whiner, but I'm just tired of feeling…" She began to search for words. "I'm just tired of feeling *blech* anymore. I do not feel like I used to feel when we were first married."

Jane was taking a big risk by just saying this to me. When she had slightly broached the subject with her mother, she encountered what she perceived to be a patronizing tone and an admonition that expecting to still feel like a newlywed after ten years of marriage was completely unrealistic. Not finding all that much help in the "cowboy up and deal with it" approach offered by her mom, she approached a friend. Jane began hesitantly and faltered halfway in. Convinced that her friend would judge her (perhaps subconsciously), she pondered each word and inflection. She honestly feared that her marriage was on the rocks and she wanted to know how to rescue it. Instead of finding a listening ear, Jane found someone else telling her where she was wrong. Her friend began to correct her perceptions about her husband. Jane instantly felt like her friend was talking over her instead of listening to her or hearing her.

Jane and Robert had met in college. They started out hot and heavy. Married a year later, they moved for his job. While they didn't like his job or the location, they loved each other deeply. Robert had a commitment to his employer for another three years. They had paid for part of his schooling, and he owed them the time for that reason. Jane figured that anyone should be able to endure almost anything for that amount of time. Besides, the money Robert made wasn't bad. It wasn't great, but it certainly provided for them better than many people she knew. While there was a lot of stress, Jane figured things would settle down when Robert was doing something he loved and not stuck in a job he hated.

The day finally came for Robert to leave his current job. He found a job working with at-risk kids where Jane could help him and they could do it together. Things started out well at the new job. Robert was having fun and helping kids. Jane was a part of it and their family was growing.

Problems soon came, though. Robert's boss seemed almost psychotic. He would task Robert with a job and then when Robert would complete the task, he would either outright attack it or point out a thousand ways that Robert could do it better. Robert started to travel all the time and although Robert's employer spoke often of family values, it seemed to Jane that recruitment was a bigger value. Whenever Jane would broach the subject with her friends, she was admonished to be thankful that Robert had a job. Of course, she was thankful, but she also wanted to feel connected to her husband. She didn't believe that was too much to ask for, but she didn't know how to get it, either.

Eventually, Robert had enough and came to her one day with a bad look on his face. He had lost his job. His employer had let him go and given them thirty days of pay. The search for a new job commenced immediately. None were found. Instead, Robert, Jane, and their three boys moved into her family's house. Taking over the basement, they continued to look for work but found none.

If you have ever lived with family, you know that privacy is hard. Every little fight that a couple might have that is forgotten three hours later may be remembered by one of the family members. There is no place to escape to in those moments of high stress for processing. Everything from how you interact with your spouse to your parenting skills is open to examination. In short, living with family is one of the hardest things that a couple can endure.

Robert finally found a job just a few hours away from her family. Far enough away that they would have some freedom they had been lacking for the last year, but close enough that their boys would be able to see her parents regularly. This was a win-win situation. Robert would be working in a more formal setting with children and youth. He would be able to do a job he loved and he should have more than enough time to spend with the family. Jane was certain she was about to get what she had been missing out on for all these years. She was about to get her husband back. Hope ran anew in her veins.

Then they moved.

Soon, Robert was working all the time again. He was surrounded by idiots and a broken system *again*. Secretly, Jane began to wonder if maybe Robert was looking at the wrong person. Maybe he was the problem. Whatever was going on, she still didn't feel connected to Robert and in her mind, that was the most important thing to accomplish. She just didn't know how. It seemed to her that the only thing Robert needed from her was sex, but she needed more. Whenever her husband was feeling particularly amorous, she would find one reason or another to not be "in the mood." A new baby put demands on her sleeping schedule and her emotional resources. Jane was scared that her marriage would end in divorce like her own parents, or maybe she would just have to live in an emotionally dead relationship.

"I don't want to sound like a crazy person, but I need more from Robert than just sex. It's so hard when it feels like that is all he wants from me."

"Jane, why do you feel like that would make you sound like a crazy person?" I asked. "Having needs met is one of the biggest benefits of marriage. In fact, I'd be willing to say that it's one of the main benefits of marriage. We are hard-wired to seek those benefits."

She looked at me with eyes afraid to hope. One single tear escaped her left eye and scurried down her cheek to disappear into the black abyss of space she felt around her. Instinctively, she crossed her arms, hugging herself as she cast her gaze to the ground. More signs of embarrassment and guilt. Jane had been hurt by her parents' divorce. She had been hurt by her husband's unwillingness to holistically connect with her. She certainly wasn't going to allow me to get too close. She was not going to allow me to build up her hope like a balloon only to have it popped by the pins of life.

"Jane, I'm curious: do you feel like Robert values you?" She looked at me blankly, wiping a bit of snot and tears off her face. "Do you feel that Robert feels like you value him?" She nearly withdrew into herself, afraid that the judgmental me was about to come out and crush her. "Do you feel that Robert hears you? Do you feel that anyone has ever heard you?"

The conversation began to really pick up now. Spurred on by the faint flickering hope that someone might actually understand where she was coming from, she began to speak faster and faster. She opened up about her father; she talked about her mom and brothers. She talked about Robert and how he never listened to her. I let her talk for nearly thirty minutes without saying anything. Finally, as though she was a ship that had survived a category-five hurricane, she took a deep breath and stopped talking. She tried to look at me and not be obvious about looking at me. I knew this would be the trickiest part of our conversation.

"Jane, do you think that Robert feels heard by you? How do you think losing his job and having to move in with your family made him feel?"

"I don't know, but it doesn't mean he should be pulling away from me!" Her anger spoke more to her fear than her anger. Anger is what therapists call a secondary emotion. It almost always masks another emotion. Often, that emotion is fear. Her eyes took an almost animalistic look as she dared me to judge her like her mom and her friend. It was my belief that she was afraid I wasn't going to help her, but that I was actually going to judge her and give her one more way she had messed up and made another mistake. The tricky part would come from the fact that I *did* believe there were probably things she could do differently, but not that she had made a mistake or done something wrong. The truth is that I believed she was living in her relationship exactly as she had been taught to live by the people around her. We give more education to people learning to flip burgers than we typically do for people who are about to get married.

"I agree, it does not, but the fact is that he isn't here

so I can't talk to him. You are here so I can only talk to you. What I'm trying to say is that I wonder if it is normal to expect that you and Robert are after the same thing in your relationship. I wonder if it isn't also safe to assume that Robert actually needs far more than sex from you—he just doesn't know how to go about getting it. It would seem reasonable to me that Robert got married to you because he loved you and he was looking forward to spending his life with his soul mate. I wonder if he isn't withdrawn from you because he is afraid that you will judge him if he were to actually share with you."

"Well, I've never judged him. Not once."

This was actually good. She was buying into the theory even if she was trying to prove that it was completely wrong in her situation.

"That may be true, and it may not be true. But what if he feels that you will? What if he feels that you have in the past? Maybe his parents judged him when he tried to be heard. Certainly his former boss judged him. I guarantee you that he feels judged by society. I would be willing to bet you good money, Jane, that he feels judged by almost every area of his life. Without ever meeting him, I'd be willing to suggest that losing his job and having to move into your family's house brought with it feelings of self-judgment and failure. Maybe he's just waiting for you to be like everyone else and judge him. Maybe he's afraid of the very things that scare you and the only way he actually feels connected to you as his wife is through sex. After all, he's been conditioned his whole life to believe that a woman will only give herself to a man that she feels connected to. I wonder if he isn't afraid that you view him as a failure and sex is his way of not feeling that way. I know I've just thrown a lot of 'I wonders' at you. What do you think?"

Her lip quivered as she responded, "So you're saying that he probably feels as disconnected as I do?"

"I don't know, but it would seem to me to be a logical conclusion. I believe that most of us have this babbling brook—this inner voice that becomes almost white noise—but we hear the message. That message is that we are all screwing up, that we are not enough. Have you ever told him how you are feeling or asked how he is feeling?"

"Well, no."

"Why not?"

She shrugged. "Simple: he's busy. He doesn't need a crazy wife dragging him down."

This is the greatest lie that most of us buy into when we hit trouble spots with our relationships. We answer for the other person in our head. We assume that we know what they would say if we were to actually talk to them. Of course, we do not know. We think we know and we react according to our perception of how they will react. This puts the other person into a bind that he or she cannot get out of. Conversations that only occur in your head not only create barriers in real life, but they also create potentially destructive defense mechanisms, because you are reacting to something that did not actually happen. You create phantom conversations because of how past real-life conversations have gone.

Do you see the insidiousness of this? By having a phantom conversation that didn't actually occur, you box the other person in. You refuse to create room for them to grow and change. Maybe they will act the same way again. Of course, the opposite is also true. Maybe they won't. Maybe they will begin the change process. Maybe this will be the time that they actually start to make progress.

Of course, this brings me to the next risk you must take. You have to realize and accept the fact that change is a process that rarely, if ever, happens overnight. It is not a linear-step process. Often, when a person is learning a new communication process, he will move nicely toward his goal and then without any particular rhyme or reason, he will digress. This is true of all of us. It is when he digresses that he hurts you again. If you are to experience everything that your heart is actually longing for, you must be willing to risk that hurt. You must be willing to love in spite of it.

It was this risk that I was encouraging Jane to enter. More than that, however, I was inviting Jane to examine her own life and how she might be able to answer Robert's core questions before she sought to have her own answered. This probably seems backward to many. But the truth is that Robert was not in the room and even if he were in the room, Jane had no way of changing him. She can only change herself. She can only work on the areas that are part of her life. Part of working on those areas will be eventually telling Robert what she needs; but for now, I will settle for her asking him how he is feeling and expressing how she is feeling. We have to give everyone the opportunity to change. We have to find healthy ways to express our own feelings and desires. Often, we express our feelings, but we do it in a way that does not create a listening environment for the person we are talking to.

Too often, my words put my wife on the defensive. Then, I get mad because she was defensive. If the person you are talking to is not hearing the words because she feels you are attacking her, the quality or rightness of your words do not matter.

Sometimes, we avoid talking about our feelings because we are afraid of conflict or we have been conditioned by society to ignore our feelings.

Eventually, our emotions build up inside of us like a balloon taped to a spigot turned on full. The balloon stretches and stretches, finally the smallest pinhole develops, and the entire thing explodes, spewing water everywhere. The water of our analogy is relatively easy to clean up, but the mess of relationships that have had explosions occur is far from easy. Often that mess will create a loop that traps and enslaves us to more negative interactions. Have you ever wondered what it would be like to engage in stress with your partner and not have the mess?

Chapter 11:

The Three Core Questions

Am I Being Heard?

Today, people are desperate to be heard. In a world that is more connected than ever (and I love technology), we feel less heard than ever. We all seek to be heard beyond simply the words that we are speaking. We want to know that the other person is hearing our heart. We want to feel there is someone who is so interested in us that they want to know the thoughts, feelings, and emotions behind the words we are speaking. We want to know that we are loved so much that someone wants to understand what we are trying to say, not simply what is coming out.

What does it mean to hear someone? To truly hear them? Often, couples tell me they feel they can't talk to their spouse and that they need to improve their communication, but they don't know what that actually means. What I find is that they simply do not feel heard. They feel like they are talking, but they don't feel like their spouse is hearing or understanding them.

They engage in a verbal ping-pong match. One partner starts talking and the other partner listens long enough to find the spot where they can throw in their own counter argument. Sometimes, they interrupt the first person. Because of this interruption, they weren't done talking so they don't wait for the other person to finish—they simply talk over the person. The stakes are raised in tone and words. Escalation increases along with anger and hurt. Guilt, shame, and fear get thrown at each other like verbal grenades. The argument becomes about winning.

By winning, I mean the goal becomes for their partner to be wrong and for said partner to admit that they are right. The effects on the relationship are devastating. The goal is not improving the relationship and building it up in a way that allows it to flourish; rather, the goal of winning actually works against the health of the relationship.

Sometimes there are no words. This is a simple truth that happens all the time. The human psyche is complex. Our emotions can override our ability to actually say the words we want to be saying. We don't know how to communicate all the time and we all want to know that there is someone who knows us so well that they will be able to put words to our feelings when we cannot.

We don't need them to fix us. We often don't even need them to fix a problem. We just absolutely need to know that they *hear* us. We need to be secure in the fact that there is at least one person who can know us so well that they can hear the lyrics of our soul. Think about couples who are intuitive to each other. They can finish each other's sentences. A simple nod can communicate volumes from one to the other. A stolen glance. These nonverbal communications begin with verbal communications. They begin with spending copious amounts of time together listening to each other.

When people tell me they have "fallen out of love" with their spouse and "fallen in love" with their new whoever, I always ask which person is getting more of their time. Invariably, I hear that the person they have fallen in love with is getting the lion's share of the time. Hearing a person tells them that they are important (which answers the valued question as well). More importantly, it tells them that someone cares about them enough to seek to understand them.

How many times in your life have you felt misunderstood or not understood at all?

Have you ever met someone who not only understood you but really *tried* to understand you? Isn't it amazing when that happens?

My guess is that your number of people who have really heard you is minimal. I would further posit that you want your spouse to be on that list and that you want to be on that list for your spouse. But how do you do that? How do you act in such a way toward your spouse that you create an environment where he or she can say, "Yes, I am heard and my partner is the one who hears me"?

CHANGE THE GOAL

The first thing you need to do is change the goal. If you truly want your spouse to feel like you hear them, you have to commit to it. You have to commit to hearing them no matter what happens. You have to commit to actions that will help you hear them better. Those actions have to help you move toward understanding your partner even if it means you won't feel like you were heard (at first). The goal has to be to improve the relationship above everything else.

Imagine if there was a fire in your house. What would you get out first? At my house, the joke is that I would grab my Mac and my iPad and then the family. Little does my wife know that with the iCloud, I have all the data so I'd let the electronics burn and get the family. Seriously, though: Would you spend time trying to figure out how the fire started while it was raging around you? Would you stand in your bedroom and try to make sure blame was assigned? What if it was your fault? Would you stand there with flames licking at your heels and attempt to deflect the blame away? I doubt it. Your only goal would be to get your loved ones and yourself out of that house.

In your relationship, when you enter into the circle of conflict, your only goal should be to understand your partner. This is primary. After that happens, you can spend time on other goals, such as how to resolve this conflict, making sure your perspective is heard, and so on.

DENY, DISMISS, AND DIMINISH

When you are having discussions with your spouse, you are often tempted to deny, dismiss, or diminish what the other person is saying. These three strategies allow you not to engage what they are saying. It creates a false sense of safety and indignity. By using them, you hurt the relationship and temporarily tell your partner that you do not care enough about them to engage what they are saying.

Couples often flat out deny what they are saying. "I told you that you needed to be there at five," is met with, "No, you didn't." And that's a flat denial. The problem with denial is that it embraces the idea of mutual blame and moves the conversation from "How do we move this relationship forward to health?" to "Who do we blame and how much blame must they accept?"

Denying is finality. It's designed to end a conversation, not to foster one. It tells the speaker that they are wrong and need to cease speaking. It kills emotional security. Denying is a deadly poison to a relationship.

DISMISS

On the surface, dismissal can look like denying. In fact, they often run hand in hand. Dismissal deals with how the other person is feeling or thinking. Your partner might tell you that he is feeling like you are neglecting him and you might respond with, "Well, that's silly." You're dismissing not only how he feels, but also the fact that he has those feelings. You are dismissing his right to the feeling. It conveys the idea that somehow we are the ones who grant or withhold permission from those we love to feel their feelings.

So, here's my question: How does a person respond to that? What would you do? What have you done when someone says that to you? Does it cause you to want to engage the person in a deep and meaningful manner? Do you want to process through the dark emotions with someone who has set himself up as your emotional priest?

Dismissal is insidious because it cuts the relationship at its most tenuous and necessary spot: the emotions. It creates a false hierarchy of worth between you and your partner. Only a person who has more worth than I do can tell me whether or not I'm allowed to feel what I'm feeling.

DIMINISH

I hate when I see someone diminishing their spouse's statements or feelings because it tends to be more subtle than the flat-out denial or dismissal. It sounds as though the spouse is actually listening when he or she is not. Its violence comes not explicitly, but implicitly.

It's violent because at first it sounds like the person might actually be listening. They might be taking the time to truly hear what you are saying and the emotions you are trying to get them to understand. In reality, they are just diminishing your feelings or thoughts. This is doubly hurtful because it brings pain twice. First, it hurts because the person is acting as though what you are saying isn't important. Secondly, hurt comes from disappointment with the fact that you thought they were trying to truly hear you and they were not. This double pain often leads to anger.

The question of being heard is foundational to a healthy relationship. We are all desperate to know that someone hears us. We want to be heard from the depths of our souls. We want to know that there is someone who is willing to wade into the murky depths of our confusion and hurt so that they can understand us.

Every person in your life is asking this question, "Am I heard?" Your spouse is no different. She wants to know that you care to hear what's on her heart as much you want to hear about your favorite sports team.

Your husband wants to know that you hear him even when he ventures into topics where he doesn't know the answer.

Unfortunately, throughout our life, we learn to deny, dismiss, or diminish issues we find uncomfortable. This works against emotional security.

You can change that by doing the hard work of truly listening. When you attempt to plumb the depths of what your partner is telling you, you will build relational equity. Your relationship builds momentum in its movement toward emotional security.

Am I Being Valued?

When you do the hard work of listening, you begin to convey to your partner that you value him or her. In many ways, you transition from listening to hearing by adding the skill of valuing your spouse.

There are so many things that are vying for our attention. So many things that demand that we stop and give them time. Sometimes, we get so caught up in those things that we fail to value those closest to us.

Beth and Ron

"Here's the thing, I give and I give to this relationship and he just doesn't value me." Beth's face streamed with tears as she talked. "If the neighbor calls, or someone at work needs him, he's up and at it right away. We could be out to dinner and have had plans for six weeks or more... if that... damn phone rings or buzzes or whatever! Boom! Up and away goes Super Ron. But if I need him to do something, well, I'm just out of luck."

Ron's eyes were almost rolling back into his head to the point that I could see the whites of his eyes. He obviously had something to say about Beth's statements. Can you guess what they were? If you guessed that he felt Beth did not value him, you are the winner.

"Look, man, my job requires that I be on call two times a month." At this point, Beth tried to interrupt him, but he talked over her. "And for the last few months, we've only had me in the department because Chad left. So, if I'm on call and the phone buzzes, I have to go fix the problem, no matter where we are or what we are doing. That's just part of the gig."

"And yes, I go help other people," he continued. "That's the right thing to do. Besides, the stuff at home will always be there. Once I get done with something that she wants me to do, guess what! She'll have more. 'Cut the grass.' Grass cut. 'Now wash the siding, now scrub the screens. The kids' bedroom door isn't level and needs fixed right now.'"

At this point, Beth was squirming in her seat. She could not believe what she was hearing. She felt she gave Ron a lot of room to do what he wanted and it was only fair that she asked him to do a little bit around the house. She worked too. And besides, when he did things, she felt loved and valued. She had just been to one of my marriage conferences and the part about being valued really stood out to her.

Let's leave Beth and Ron there for a moment.

We all need to feel valued. It's an inherent part of our nature and many volumes have been written discussing this need. The problem is that we all feel valued in different ways. On the one hand, we all know people make time for the things they value and we often spend money on those things. Even with this knowledge, we still have disagreements about what it means to value someone and these disagreements often lead to many arguments in relationships.

Beth and Ron were both frustrated. They both felt as though their actions should be conveying that their spouse was important to them. The problem was that they were doing things that they felt value from. They expected their spouse to feel value from the same actions that they felt value from. Ron felt most valued when he was *told* he was valued. Beth felt most valued when someone *spent time* with her. They expected the other person to receive value in the same way that they did. This would be like Beth liking spaghetti and expecting Ron to like it because she likes it. Almost no one expects their partner to like all of the same foods, but many people expect their partner to feel valued in the same way that they feel value.

This problem usually becomes further complicated because often, both people feel they are not valued and the strategies they employ to express that push their partner away, destroying any sense of safety in the relationship. This loss of safety results in more actions that do not work and less value being shared between the couple.

"Ron, are you saying that you don't feel like Beth values what you do?" I asked as I tentatively began to join them in the rapidly escalating conversation. Beth began to object to my asking the question, but I explained to her that clarification was one of the best skills we could develop if we were going to be good communicators. It is imperative that we create safety for our partner and ourselves by making sure that we understand what is being said and communicated before we respond. This gives us a better chance of avoiding hurtful miscommunication.

"Heck yes, I'm saying that! She never says, 'Thanks' or 'Hey, I appreciate that.' I get more thanks at work."

"Why in God's green earth should I thank you for doing something that has to be done?" Beth's retort rushed after his like a tumbleweed caught in a gale force wind.

"Because it's a nice thing to hear. Maybe because it's kind!"

"Well, no one thanks me for doing what I have to do!"

"Oh, really! That's not even true. I just told you thank you for bringing me that converter the other day."

"Well, that isn't something I *have* to do, so I would expect it there!" Suddenly, Beth looked at me. "You know what I mean?" she asked me with a sincere expression and some confusion.

That confusion grew when I told her that I wasn't sure that I *did* understand what she meant.

"Well, cleaning the windows or mowing the lawn are things that have to be done. My taking him a converter on my day off for his job isn't something I have to do. To me, the stuff he's talking about is like doing laundry or cooking for me. He doesn't thank me for it, and I'm okay with that. I don't expect it. I do expect that he'll do his part."

"Beth, are you saying that he shouldn't expect you to say thanks because you don't expect him to say it for the same types of activities?"

Now Beth looked at me with an extremely perplexed look on her face. "Well, I just don't think that my saying thanks for that kind of stuff shows him that I value him."

Beth and Ron were both committing one of the most common fallacies I see in relationships. They were assuming that the other person should see the situation exactly as they see it. This causes a vicious loop of engagement that is painful, leading to an unhealthy retreat. The result is hurt feelings and a lack of safety.

The good news is that you cannot make your spouse feel valued. You can only create fertile ground where feeling valued grows. This is because it is impossible to make your spouse feel anything. We are still responsible, though, to hear what they are saying and when possible, incorporate the expressed response or action into our life.

In other words, regardless of how Beth feels about words being a legitimate source of feeling valued, she needs to consider using those words because Ron told Beth that he would feel valued in this way. She does not have to automatically incorporate this activity into her life, but she does need to hear it. She can't decide what she is going to do until she truly hears what he is asking. Notice that value comes from hearing, which is why I led with the question of being heard.

If she decides that she cannot thank him for doing things around the house, she needs to utilize good conversational skills with Ron to explain that decision. Simply saying, "I don't think I should have to do that because it seems stupid to me" is not going to be helpful to creating emotional security in the relationship. Part of valuing someone means that we will do something simply because it is important to them.

Conversely, Ron needs to really take the time to hear Beth. Most of the time, it seems to me that people—especially men—feel like they are doing a good job valuing their spouse. Because of this belief, they tend to outright deny their partner's claim that they are not valuing them. This leads to more anger and resentment, choking the emotional security of the relationship.

He might mirror her and incorporate some clarifying questions into his response with her. Giving her the opportunity to express what she believes has been happening and what is wrong with the current situation. Most importantly, he needs to ask her what it would like to do it the way she's wanting him to.

What would it look like to Beth for his actions to show her that he valued her? This would allow Ron to better understand her perspective and what she is looking for in the relationship. Once he has that understanding, he can decide if he is able to provide that interaction to Beth or not. If he cannot, he will need to tell her in a safe and truthful manner.

TIME AND MONEY

We get to vote for what we value with two things for what we value: how we spend our time and our money. Even in the example of Beth and Ron. Ron is asking her to spend her time saying thank you. If you want to know what you value, look at where you spend your time and money.

I enjoy reading. If you looked at my spending habits and my use of time, you would come to that conclusion quickly. I have audiobooks, digital books, and paper books strewn everywhere in my life.

Conversely, I do not value fishing. I have spent very little time or money on the activity in my entire life. I don't mind talking with people who enjoy fishing, but I'm not interested in spending any of my resources on it.

I value having a wide base of knowledge in order to be able to talk with and connect to my clients. I do not value the NFL. However, I stay abreast of the news and activities of that league so that I can live out the value of connecting with clients and coworkers.

The end of the calendar year is coming to a close as I write these words. I have already begun making arrangements for my wife and I to have dates next calendar year. The dates of these activities go into my calendar before anything else. Tickets are bought, hotels reservations made, etc.

I do this because I believe that these getaway times are important. I value her and our relationship. I'm demonstrating this with my time and money. If my words are divorced from my actions, my words are meaningless. Incidentally, there was a time when we could not afford to go away. I voted with my money by paying my bills and I voted with my time by going for walks with her or going on dates that didn't cost anything.

Most of us have some discretionary funds and time. If we're not dedicating some of that to our spouse, we are not demonstrating that we value them.

When you combine truly hearing your partner with valuing her, you begin the process of showing her she is safe with you. In the next chapter, I will look at what it means to be safe.

AM I SAFE?

One of the most perplexing issues that any relationship will face is the need to create safety. Relationally speaking, safety comes from engaging in what most people perceive to be the most dangerous activity. Namely, safety comes from repeatedly engaging in vulnerability. Of course, most people have a war raging inside of them between their desire to be intimate (defined here as being emotional naked) and their desire not to be hurt. Because of this, they will often engage in destructive behaviors that work against the health of the relationship.

Most people desperately want someone to hear them, but they are afraid that being heard isn't safe. Imagine if I gave you two sheets of paper: one red and one green. On the red paper, I asked you to write down everything you dislike about yourself or everything that you wish you could change. Once that list is done, please continue with everything about yourself that you feel is odd or does not fit into society at large as "normal." Now, on the green paper, please write down everything you love about yourself. The stuff that you cannot wait to share with the whole world. Now, write down everything about yourself that you have never once thought needed to be changed.

Which sheet has the longer list? Which sheet takes longer to fill out? Which sheet has answers that jump out of you? Which sheet has answers that you ponder the wisdom of putting down on paper? Most people would have a much easier time coming up with answers for the red (negative) sheet and many would worry about putting those answers down where someone else could find them and read them.

We are all subconsciously seeking to find someone with whom we can share both of those sheets. This is the heart of intimacy: letting someone see all of you—the good, the bad, the cool, the ugly, the gorgeous—and receiving an affirmation to the question, "Can you still love me?" We all seek to find safety before we attempt to be vulnerable. A person skilled in building intimate relationships with those she cares about will be able to create safety in increments.

Being safe means that your past is not used to hurt you in a fight. Being safe means that you are willing to engage in conflict with your spouse to better your relationship because the relationship is more important to you than comfort. Being safe means that you do not try to make your spouse pay over and over again for past indiscretions. Being safe flows out of being heard and valued because you protect those things that you value.

Sadly, for most of us, we are taught at an early age that we are not safe to share many things. Our deepest dreams are shot down as impractical by well-meaning teachers, mentors, or even parents. I watch children being verbally attacked by their parents for being children and wonder what that child's mental dialogue will be as an adult. Hurtful words are said in a moment of anger. The following apology does little to repair the crater of pain left in that child's heart.

In an effort to fit in, students split into self-regulated peer groups. Children who may strike up a friendship outside of school settings may not be able to engage that friendship because of unwritten societal rules inside the school. Incidentally, if we ever meet in a coffee shop, let's talk about the idea behind modern schooling, segregation based on age and the effect it is having on our children's mental and emotional development.

All of these interactions tell us in both explicit and implicit ways that we are rarely safe. Absent and abusive parents add to the lesson. This message coagulates in our heart like rapidly drying cement, and many people subconsciously make a pact with themselves to never be too vulnerable. Simultaneously, they desperately seek intimacy.

In the next chapter, I will look at four distinct negative patterns that we tend to use in our relationships. In an effort to get the very thing we want most in our relationships, these patterns actually stop us from it. They seem to offer protection, but often they leave us alone and hurt. When I talk to people about these patterns, they often recognize them right away. Sometimes, they do not want to give them up. Instead, like a long-held secret lover, they embrace them. They actually get angry when it is suggested that they will need to give up on these patterns. If you recognize these patterns, you know they are destructive. They will tear at the heart of your relationship. They will not fulfill you. They will undermine all of your other efforts to build trust and love in your partner.

Recognizing the problem is the first part of the problem. Learning a strategy to change it is the next step. I invite you to discuss what you read in these chapters with your spouse or partner.

Chapter 12:

Four Emotional Hazards

JOHN SIPPED HIS COFFEE, REMEMBERING HIS argument with Katrina.

"I finally just told her that I'm tired of always being the bad guy. She gets in a mood and that's it. I'm the problem—it's never her fault."

I couldn't help but wonder how this line of approach worked for John. Did he get what he was looking for in his relationship with his wife? So I asked him, "I'm curious how that worked out for you. Did she stop blaming you? Did your relationship improve?"

He looked at me as if I had suddenly grown too many heads to count. Staring at me as though I were some sort of mythical hydra hell-bent on his destruction, he physically recoiled deeper into his seat. "What do you mean? Did it work?"

"Well, we all do the things we do so that we can achieve something. Just like you exchanged money for the shoes you are wearing, you spoke those words to your wife, hoping to get something from her in return. For instance, you may have wanted her to stop talking to you that way. Or you may have wanted her to see your perspective on the issue. There are dozens of potential things you wanted to see happen from you sharing those words with her. I'm wondering if you know what it was that you wanted and if you got that from her when you spoke those words to her."

John looked at me with more bewilderment. "What do you mean, like right then?" His voice rose at the end with his increased incredulousness. "Of course not. I mean, not right then. I actually think she got angrier, which is completely stupid if you ask me. I was just telling her how I feel. Everything is such a huge deal with her. I get tired of it."

John continued to vent his frustrations to me over what he believed were the many problems with his wife. There was conflict every day it seemed since, well, forever. No matter what John did for her, it seemed to turn out wrong. The silliest thing would end up in a shouting match for hours. Threats of divorce would ring out like fireworks on the Fourth of July. John felt as though Katrina was always trying to get a reaction from him. He was tired of always feeling like everything was his fault. If he tried to comfort his wife, she would pull away. If he tried to give her comfort, she would rage about how withdrawn he was from her. No matter what he did, he felt like it never worked out. He sincerely believed that if he could just figure out "how to fix whatever was wrong with her," things in their marriage would turn around.

KATRINA'S POINT OF VIEW

Katrina was incredulous. She looked at Mary as though she had just confessed to the deepest, darkest secret of her life. "There is no way you actually expect me to apologize to him when all he did was his job!"

Katrina was angry and hurt. She and John seemed to be constantly fighting over everything. Yesterday, John arrived home before her like he always did and cleaned the house. Of course, the bathroom didn't look like she wanted it to and the kitchen wasn't exactly worthy of a white-glove inspection, but he had cooked a fairly simple meal. Cooking is actually too much credit—all he did was microwave some vegetable trays and make macaroni and cheese. Then he had the nerve to expect her to thank him for his effort. What—as if he thanked her when she came home and cooked? He just expected it of her and now because he actually got up off of that stinking chair one time, he expected her to fall over herself thanking him? That was absolutely ridiculous. The more he talked to her, the more she felt underappreciated until she had had enough. Finally, she blew up at him and used her words to protect herself as she always does.

Predictably, John shut down and stopped talking

to her altogether. That was just like him. He never actually engaged her with his emotions until he was really good and angry. Then, of course, his words came out in torrents, tumbling over each other faster than rushing water. Oh sure, he's great at paying the bills and providing, but Katrina wanted more. She wanted a partner. She wanted someone who invited her into his life. John was never much of a conversationalist and he certainly never did anything much around the house; but with the kids and work, she needed some help. Even more, she needed someone who knew who she was. It just felt as though John had no idea who she was anymore. She used to cry over it, but the time for crying was done. She was tired of putting her emotions out there and getting nothing.

Why couldn't John be like Frank at work? Frank was such a good listener. When she talked to him, she felt as if he were peering into her soul, hanging onto her every word. He cared about who she was and what mattered to her. Of course, John didn't like her talking to Frank and he certainly didn't like her chatting with him on Facebook. Well, too bad for John. It wasn't like she was going to sleep with Frank or anything like that. Of course, everything always comes back to sex for John. He could be angry with her and could be in a death match from Hades but two hours later, he would decide he was horny and want her to give herself to him. Well, no way. She may not have control over many things, but she certainly could control what she did with her own body. Sex with a stranger was no fun at all. She was tired of feeling like some sort of sex toy for John's pleasure. This was not what she signed up for when she got married. And now Mary agreed with John! She wanted Katrina to thank him! She was probably just trying to cause problems between her and John for her own gain. What kind of friend would take his side?

DANGEROUS CONVERSATIONS

John and Katrina were living in what I call dangerous conversations. They were living in an emotionally hazardous land that was wreaking havoc on them. They were caught in a perilous cycle of engagement that ended in pain. They were hoping for intimacy but were caught in habits that were detrimental to the emotional security of their relationship. This loss of emotional security destroyed any chance they had at intimacy. Let's look at another example of Hannah and Alex.

Hannah took a deep breath as she pulled her car into the garage. It had been a long day. Her boss had been all over her about a project with a deadline that had come and gone. She had felt distracted all day. On the way home, she had gotten a speeding ticket.

She knew her husband Alex wasn't going to be happy. *She* wasn't happy! They had been saving for months for a new truck. They had put together an incredibly tight budget and had been throwing money into their savings account.

Alex could be so rigid sometimes. He saw the world his way and that was pretty much the only way it worked. He was a great guy, but sometimes he acted like he was her dad. She had already felt like he was being a bit of a money Nazi. This was only going to make it worse.

Now, there was going to be a fine to pay and their insurance was going to go up. Car insurance in their state was already high. She really wasn't in the mood to deal with his crap tonight. It wasn't like she meant to get the stupid ticket. These thoughts and a thousand others swirled through her brain as she put the car in park and opened the door, only to hear it hit the side of Alex's car, causing a dent.

Inside the house, Alex was wiping down the table as quickly as possible. He had been roasting coffee beans and didn't want Hannah to come home to a messy house. He knew she hated that. Inside, he was angry. He figured she was angry too, though. They had been going to couples counseling for a little while and one of the things the counselor had helped him understand was the fact that he could do better at seeing things from Hannah's point of view.

They didn't have the money for this stupid ticket. He wished she would be more responsible—well, not really more responsible. She was actually very responsible. She just wasn't always… connected! She just wasn't always *connected*. He heard her car pull into the garage.

I hope she parks under the tennis ball I hung for her, he thought absently as he placed the cloth over the kitchen sink. He had hung a tennis ball in the garage when he had bought his new-to-them car. Hannah had a habit of parking too closely to his old car and she would hit his door when she got out. With the old beater, it didn't really matter that much; but with the new car, he really wanted to keep it from becoming a beater. Nothing seemed to work so he had parked her car in the right spot and hung a tennis ball from a string attached to the ceiling. When her car was parked just right, the tennis ball would touch the windshield right in front of her face. Then she could open the door and get out with a couple of inches to spare. He had been pretty proud of himself that day.

As he was opening the door, he heard her door hit his car. "Why didn't you park where I showed you?" he asked plaintively.

Her face showed him immediately that this was the wrong thing to say, but he didn't care. *She just doesn't care about money like she should.*

WHAT ARE THE EMOTIONAL HAZARDS?

We all run the risk of becoming caught in a dangerous conversation. Relationships are inherently risky. The very thing we want the most will often terrify us. As we begin to move deeper into a relationship, we want to be heard, valued, and safe. The paradox is that we have to risk when trying to achieve these things. Most couples have learned that risk is dangerous so they bail on the idea, or worse, they sabotage the relationship. Typically, couples fight in destructive patterns. This is probably because we tend to teach our children about everything except how to be in a relationship. We teach our children (probably unintentionally) that all conflict is bad and destructive. This leaves us with adults who are often emotionally stunted and have no idea how to navigate the hazards in relationships.

Typically, couples will stumble through four emotional hazards:

- Negative feedback loop (It all goes wrong, all the time)
- Finding the bad guy (Mutual blame)
- Hunting and running (Not blowing up and shutting down)
- Sitting out (What's the point, anyway?)

Andrew was a student of mine at a small private school. Because the school was on a tight budget, many of the male teachers doubled as parking lot attendants in the mornings. One morning, I was putting the orange cones out that were part of the daily routine when a little white truck came screeching into the parking lot. It was obviously in a gear that was a little low for the speed it was going. Later that morning as we were preparing for class, I mentioned to him that I heard him coming this morning before I saw him and I mentioned that he might want to shift up in the future or slow down (my real goal was for him to slow down).

He immediately replied, "Well, I heard you almost stalled the other day on the way to the Y!" Andrew was utilizing one of the oldest ploys in the book: mutual blame. He was avoiding his own problems with his new transition to a manual transmission by pointing back at what he believed was my own inadequacy with a manual transition.

In the negative feedback loop, everything goes wrong. There is no win for either party when they are caught in this loop. No matter what they do, there is criticism and pain. This criticism and pain creates more resentment. The lens of each person in the relationship becomes fogged over with fear and cynicism.

NEGATIVE FEEDBACK LOOP

Ryan and Ashley were excited to celebrate his birthday. Ryan's favorite restaurant was a steakhouse not far from their house. Ashley crawled into the driver's seat as Ryan plopped down in the passenger seat reading an email that had just come through on his phone. About two minutes later, he looked up and asked in a calm and quiet voice, "Why are you going this way?" Later, Ashley agreed he had said that in a calm and quiet voice.

The fight that ensued lasted for over eight hours.

For eight hours, they fought over everything that happened. Taking pot shots at each other's food choices and mannerisms, they utilized their weapons of words to hurt the other person. Emotionally, they made poor decision after poor decision, setting off verbal and emotional sticks of dynamite. Their words were like termites tearing at the inside of a structure.

Obviously, this argument was about more than the statement regarding navigation choices. It was about the story in her head: what did he really mean by those words and what does he *really* think about her? We only have meaning because of the stories in our heads. But the choice to continue in the negativity was 100 percent theirs to make. It did not matter what either person said or did; they were stuck seeing everything through the negative feedback loop.

Couples in this hazard refuse to give the other person the benefit of the doubt. Their words are driven by entitlement and grandiosity. Self-justification becomes the goal of the interaction. Safety is chosen over vulnerability.

Let's break that down for a moment. When this hazard occurs, couples will often excuse their own behavior by pointing to the bad behavior of the other person. They will speak as though they are entitled to do hurtful things to the other person because the other person did hurtful things to them. This is the essence of entitlement.

It runs holding hands with grandiosity. The actions

of the other person are inflated to be beyond any hope. The pain that this person has experienced is cast to be more severe than the pain experienced by any other person. Their victim status is elevated to be higher than their guilty status. That is to say, they diminish their own responsibility while aggrandizing the pain the other person has inflicted on them. They draw lines with their words. They create hoops demanding that their partner jump through as proof of their love knowing that the hoops are impossible to jump through.

I once was called for a consult by another counselor. He was seeing a woman who had been cheating on her husband. When the husband caught her, she decided to move in with her boyfriend. So she packed up their three kids and the dog and moved into the boyfriend's house. The husband refused to file for divorce and told her that he wanted to work it out, which is how they found my friend. They both started doing individual therapy with the idea that they would move toward couples therapy. The wanted to discover how they felt about a possible reconciliation.

During these sessions, my colleague discussed what would be necessary for them to feel safe in couples therapy. One of the things the husband consistently listed was wanting his wife to move out of her boyfriend's house. She wanted him to take the dog back. He never wanted the dog but agreed to take it back, hoping it would show her his seriousness about reconciliation.

In the meantime, he decided to file for divorce, stating that they could always get remarried or that he could not file the final paperwork, allowing the proceedings to dissolve. This failure to file would render the divorce filing null and the marriage could continue. (Please remember, I'm a counselor who skipped the day they covered divorce law in law school, but this is an accurate rendition of the story related to me by my friend.) She was okay with his filing.

As the individual therapy progressed, they continued to talk about the possibility of couples counseling. The wife refused to move out of the boyfriend's house and the husband actually went on a few dates. She finally offered him an ultimatum in the form of a date and time that he was supposed to attend couples counseling. He told her that he could not make that time work because he had concert tickets that night. When asked if he was going with someone, he admitted he had a date. The concert was to see a band that both individuals had liked for many years and the tickets had been purchased by the husband before the affair was discovered. The wife was furious and actually said to my friend, "I'm just not sure that he's serious about our relationship if he can't give up his concert."

That is the epitome of entitlement and grandiosity. My friend was at his wit's end. He wanted to know what direction I thought he should take with the therapy.

To be fair, I did not know this couple. I would not recognize either of them in public, but I have seen this story repeat itself in various forms many times in the room.

The wife was diminishing her own role in the destruction of the relationship. She had not met any of the husband's requests to move into couples therapy. He had met all of hers. She self-justified by blaming her affair on circumstance, often saying, "It just happened. I wasn't looking for it." She followed that up with entitlement: "Aren't I supposed to be happy?"

In essence, everything that the husband did was wrong. The obvious danger for the husband was that he would engage in the same type of destructive behavior. In his attempts to find safety, he might be tempted to diminish everything she did as wrong or not good enough. He might create impossible expectations for her so that he can tell himself he tried to make it work despite the relationship being doomed.

For their relationship to move from unhealthy to healthy, they will both have to engage in honest vulnerability. It's good to draw boundaries, but they will need to truly be vulnerable if their relationship is going to heal. Part of that vulnerability will be to admit to their own roles in the destruction of the relationship. They will need to do that without adding any qualifiers to those admissions. Qualifiers are statements like, "I'm sorry that I withdrew from you, but you were being so unreasonable all the time."

Hopefully, your negative feedback loop isn't as severe as this couple's, but if you have been with your partner for any period, my guess is that you have experienced the negative feedback loop. One of the most common ways that couples will engage in this danger is by focusing on a detail they disagree with. They may agree with the majority of what was said, but they will fight to the death over the minority part with which they disagree. They may be willing to fight over the difference of ten minutes or three words.

"You didn't say…"

"You said…"

When they are caught in this hazard, there is very little grace available for either person. Assumptions about the other person's intent usually turn cynical and drift toward the worst possible conclusions. Their spouse is held to the exact letter of what they said or did, even if they immediately stated that they didn't mean to say something that way or do it that way. If there is a choice to be made in how an action or word can be viewed, the choice is almost always negative when someone is caught in the negative feedback loop.

The negative feedback highlights how activities we engage in because we think they will create safety actually create danger for our relationships. Because this hazard begins all of the other loops we will talk about, it is imperative that we train ourselves to recognize our use of it as the dangerous defense mechanism that it is.

Finding the Bad Guy (Mutual Blame)

When couples are caught in this emotional hazard, they have a lot of dangerous conversations that revolve around blame. They tend to fight over who was and is at fault rather than look at how they can move forward. They will often use phrases like the following:

"Don't blame me here—I'm not the bad guy!" or "I am so sick of you doing _____. If you would just do _____. I am tired of always being made to feel like the bad buy in this relationship."

The conversation tends to revolve around who is at fault while the other person is not the one at fault. It tends to be a conversation that is mired in sideways energy. It doesn't improve the relationship at all; it simply causes it to spin out of control. Usually, the couple cannot even agree what happened when they are caught in this emotional hazard.

The narrative becomes about finding the person to blame. The problem is not whatever is detracting from the relationship; rather, the issue becomes finding a way to blame the partner for the difficulty. When a person is stuck in the blame game, they cannot step back from the potential problem to see something beyond the hurt. It becomes about hurting the partner or justifying oneself.

This is a completely destructive communication technique because it wastes so much energy. Invariably, both people end up feeling wasted and spent emotionally. They run back and forth verbally with blame being used as a weapon. This hazard takes them away from their goal of resolving the conflict. It leaves them hurt and bleeding.

JULIE AND KEVIN

Julie and Kevin knew exactly what I was talking about when I first brought up this idea to them. They were just a few years into their marriage when Julie cheated on Kevin with a guy from her gym. In our very first session together, she spilled the proverbial beans. Immediately, Kevin berated her. He quickly engaged in the blame game. Julie had none of it. She immediately pointed out that she was certain Kevin had had multiple affairs over the course of their marriage. She pulled out printed-off emails, text messages, and Facebook interactions.

The conversation quickly devolved into a shouting match. He was calling her names, and she was telling him that he was just like his father. They were both on the attack and caught in the negative feedback loop. For a few moments, it was if I wasn't in the room anymore. They were simply screaming at each other. The windows shook with the reverberations. They quickly moved through all of the emotional hazards, except sitting out, and then that came too.

Finally spent, they both sat down on the couch and simply looked at me with a "what now?" type of look.

I asked them if perhaps the real problem had nothing to do with the affairs and perhaps had more to do with other things in their relationship. I explained to them the idea of emotional hazards. Specifically, I explained that by blaming each other, they were failing to see the real problems that were a part of their narrative.

The real problem is the lack of emotional security in the relationship. When there is no emotional security, there is no trust, love, or respect. When there is no love, trust, or respect, there is guilt, shame, and fear—the three killers of almost all relationships.

WHAT IS IT?

Finding the bad guy happens when a couple seeks to assign blame in a situation rather than working on finding a solution.

WHY IS THIS BAD?

This is a dangerous emotional hazard for three reasons:
1. It doesn't improve the relationship.
2. It causes hurt and resentment for both parties.
3. It doesn't communicate that anyone is being heard, valued, or safe.

IT DOESN'T IMPROVE THE RELATIONSHIP.

The first and biggest problem with finding the bad guy is that it doesn't help the relationship. If the marks of a healthy relationship are each party feeling heard, valued, and safe, this hazard directly threatens those characteristics. It causes each person to often feel attacked and persecuted.

IT CAUSES HURT AND RESENTMENT.

Any time someone feels attacked and persecuted, they will tend to feel resentment and hurt. This resentment and hurt will build up over time and attack the very sinews of the relationship, which causes a relationship to fall apart. Fights will tend to spiral and increase in intensity. Hurt will build like bricks in a wall, slowly forcing the couple apart. Sometimes, the relationship implodes; sometimes, it deteriorates slowly over time, dying a slow, painful death.

IT DOESN'T COMMUNICATE THAT ANYONE IS BEING HEARD, VALUED, OR SAFE.

This may seem like a no-brainer, but no one feels heard, valued, or safe when this emotional hazard is in play. Both people feel like they are being talked over and blamed for *all of the problems*. Instinctively, we know that no one is 100 percent to blame for a relationship. This hazard attacks people and often ignores the real problem that is tearing the couple apart: creating new problems. This becomes a self-feeding loop with the other hazards because the more one of the partners feels attacked, the more they will tend to see everything as going badly. The more they see things go badly, the more likely they are to go on the attack or run away (the "let's go hunting" hazard). This then creates more opportunities for blame because destructive things are being done by both people, which provides examples that can be used as weapons usually disguised as proof of guilt.

HUNTING AND RUNNING (NOT BLOWING UP AND SHUTTING DOWN).

You probably know of this next hazard as "blowing up and shutting down." I am not a fan of that metaphor because the hunter may not utilize blowing up and the runner will almost always end up blowing up at some point. Let's take a look at how this hazard works.

When a hunter feels insecure, he will often utilize intensity to gain some feeling of emotional connectedness or emotional security. This may come in the form of yelling or sarcasm. It may come in the form of passive-aggressiveness, but it will almost always be destructive to the overall health of the relationship.

The runner simply shuts down when he feels distressed. He will sometimes shut down by just agreeing, but usually this is a sign of another emotional hazard. He hopes to avoid conflict by not engaging, thus feeling more secure. The hunter is hoping to feel more secure by having conflict.

Have you ever had friends who fought so much you wondered why they were together? If so, you may have had friends who were both hunters. Typically what happens is that both partners will do this dance of unhealthy engagement until they either both decide to run away from it or have a blow-up fight.

When they decide to run away from it, they often just stop talking to each other. They will tell me that they "just sweep it under the rug" and stop talking to each other for a few days. Then they start talking about something that is safe and work really hard at pretending nothing happened to cause conflict.

Despite my rule to always avoid always and never say never, this approach *never* works. It is a guaranteed recipe for resentment, anger, and hurt feelings. It brings to the couple the very thing they were hoping to avoid: emotional instability.

When a couple does this dangerous dance of hunting and running, they no longer feel safe with each other. Rather than attempting to create that safety through the hard work of good communication that builds friendship and intimacy, they attempt to shut down the uncomfortable feelings.

This is similar to setting your house on fire in order to clean it. The end result leaves you in more of a difficult situation than when you had started. It will almost always lead a couple down the path to divorce, or at the very best, intensive marriage therapy. It not only destroys emotional security, but I believe it also tears at the very soul of a person and creates feelings of loneliness, isolation, and despair.

WHAT IS IT?

"Let's go hunting" occurs when two people have a distinct way of pursuing emotional security in a bad way. One by utilizing words to attack or "hock and awe" their partner into loving them. The other by withdrawing, hiding, and refusing to engage.

WHY IS THIS BAD?

This is damaging because it actually does the exact opposite of what we are hoping it will do. Rather than creating emotional security, it hampers emotional security's ability to grow. It is attempting to create the feeling of being loved at any and all cost.

SITTING OUT (WHAT'S THE POINT, ANYWAY?)

Kyra and Garrett had been fighting for the entire afternoon. When they talked to me about it later, they were not sure what had started it, but it had covered a lot of ground topically. He had reminded her of the time she was driving and refused to listen to his advice on where to turn. She had reminded him of the time when he had an emotional affair. She pointed out how it was his fault, and he reminded her that she was doing the very things she was accusing him of doing.

Finally, she raised her hand and simply told him that he won. She was done arguing. She couldn't take another minute of it. He retorted that she didn't get to decide that and that *he* was done. She went out to the barn to brush her horse and cry, and he opened a beer and turned on the baseball game. They didn't talk for three days.

When we emotionally sit out, we just stop engaging. This happens two distinct ways. Both are destructive and dangerous because they stop relationships from growing and creating emotional security.

The first way that a couple sits out is they just stop engaging. They may have been fighting for a while. The fight has covered a lot of topics and has run around a number of past transgressions. Finally, energy runs out. Someone agrees simply because they are tired of fighting. Nothing has been resolved, but there is just this overwhelming sense that nothing can be resolved so let's just stop the fight.

You will hear phrases like, "I'm done, you win!" or "I can't do this anymore!" Whatever you hear, it's a statement of giving up, not resolution. It stops the fight and guts the relationship.

WILL AND BETH

Will and Beth had been married for twenty-two years. They had four grown children. The youngest of which was moving out of the house soon. Everyone thought they were the picture-perfect couple. They paid their bills on time, went to all the local functions, and were active as a couple in the local charity scene. A yearly family picture dominated a wall of family photos in the great room that everyone commented on during their annual community block party.

Shock rippled through the community when Will served Beth with divorce papers. Everyone, that is, except Beth. She knew that for years they had just stopped engaging. They didn't fight because they didn't actually engage. If something came up that they had to figure out, they would almost mechanically disengage like a well-maintained machine. Beyond that, they simply avoided anything beneath the surface.

They had been doing the dance of the first three emotional hazards for years. Regularly ending by giving up, which was signaled by sitting out. They did these dances until they finally started sitting out completely. They just stopped engaging. This is the second way that couples sit out and, in my opinion, it is the most dangerous.

It feels safe, especially at first. There are surface smiles and some laughter, but there is no engagement. Indeed, engagement begins to feel dangerous and unsafe. It begins to feel like the enemy.

The couple grows apart. They are good at doing

the business side of their relationship and terrible at doing the heart side of their marriage. Like a sponge deprived of water, their hearts become cracked, brittle, and shrunken. The idea of engaging in emotional vulnerability becomes terrifying.

This is destructive to the relationship because emotional vulnerability is the key to moving the relationship to health. Friendship and intimacy flow out of vulnerability, and emotional security flows out of friendship and intimacy.

WHAT IS IT?

Emotionally sitting out is when a couple disengages, not because anything has been solved but because they wish to stop the uncomfortable feelings of the engagement more than they wish to solve the problem. Over time, this will probably lead to the couple sitting out completely in the relationship. Fights will stop and disagreements will cease because the relationship is deteriorating.

WHY IS IT BAD?

Emotionally sitting out is dangerous because it communicates to your spouse that you care about your own comfort more than you care about the relationship and, in turn, more than you care about your spouse. This puts the entire relationship at risk and works against cultivating emotional safety and moving the relationship toward health. It is borne from entitlement and selfishness. Rather than providing safety, it actually creates more wounds and scars in the relationship.

Maybe you recognized parts of these emotional hazards in your own life. Anytime two people attempt to merge their lives, there will be poor behaviors. The key is to develop habits that protect the emotional life of your relationship. If the majority of interactions float through these emotional hazards, most relationships will die.

Chapter 13:

How Do We Fix It?

WHEN WE ENCOUNTER AND ENGAGE IN EMOTIONAL hazards, what do we do? How do we move beyond them? How do we fix the relationship?

One of the first steps is to change how we interact with the relationship itself. That is to say, we work on changing our assumptions and expectations about the relationship and our partner. But you may be wondering, "How do I do that?"

Change your assumptions and expectations by changing the system that you use to communicate in the relationship.

For couples to move toward each other and build the relationship, they must navigate three steps. Before we get to that, let's look at how fights happen. Rare is the fight that happens out of nowhere. Typically, they occur after each person has become more agitated throughout the day. This agitation may be with each other and it may not. One person might be escalated in their agitation because the kids did irritating things all day. The other person might be agitated because of something they read on Facebook. Regardless of whatever escalates them, couples must accomplish three things in order to be able to navigate the situation.

First, they need to be able to de-escalate themselves. Second, they need to be able to tolerate the stress of being agitated and not give into the temptation of fighting. Finally, they need to problem solve. Often, couples will attempt to go straight to problem-solving, which makes the situation worse.

De-escalate

Couples must be able to de-escalate to a space where they can talk. This allows them to tolerate the stress so that they can problem solve. Often, couples inherently have two problems with this system. First, as previously mentioned above, they want to go straight to problem-solving. Second, they tend to see fights in a vacuum. When couples discuss their fights with me, they act as though their fight came up out of nowhere and just happened. Like a fast-moving midwestern thunderstorm, the winds of change blew and a fight erupted out of nowhere.

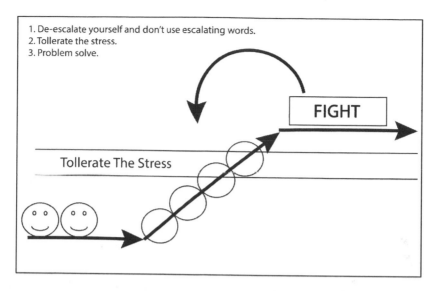

In most cases, this narrative of a fight out of nowhere is patently false. Usually, the fight builds over time. As often as not, the nefarious forces that build like a slow-moving freight train in the barometer of a relationship are not even in the control of one's partner, nor are they directly related to them. Like a small but persistent gas leak, the pressures of life build up and have nowhere to go. So they collect, until the smallest spark sets off an explosion.

Take the example of my friend Jeff. Jeff had a high-stress job that few people understood. His boss, Brian, was unpredictable and often volatile. He would berate Jeff and change Jeff's workload frequently. The last few weeks had been brutal. There was a major project going on that involved multiple teams and departments from within their organization. He had spent the better part of the last two weeks working on a major part of the project and the necessary presentation to procure funding to move the project forward.

At the last minute, Brian made some significant changes to the presentation. As you can imagine, this caused Jeff a great deal of stress. On top of that, Jeff's parents were coming for a visit the next week—and their relationship was stressful. Kate's parents, Jeff's in-laws, had just left after visiting for a week. This caused Jeff stress, because it caused Kate stress. Her father never seemed to be satisfied with anything that she did, and he let her know constantly.

Finally, Jeff had just received bad news at the doctor's regarding his health. While not a death sentence, it was going to require a lot of significant changes to his lifestyle. Jeff's stress level was high. Compounding issues, he had not eaten much on this day. Later, he would admit that he was probably somewhat "hangry." In case you're wondering, *hangry* is that wonderful space where you're not mad but everything bothers you and you feel angry about almost everything because you are hungry.

As Jeff drove home, he fantasized about decompressing. He could hear his favorite composer playing through his stereo system and envisioned the pages of the book he was going to read. Perhaps a fine glass of his favorite red wine would accompany his evening. It would be bliss and he would be able to ignore the stress of the day for a little while.

Kate had other plans for Jeff.

She had stayed home all day working from home with their three children. She had just taken her third pregnancy test and all three had come back positive. While she was excited, she was also nervous. They had just bought a new vehicle and it had fit their family of five perfectly. There was no spot for a sixth seat. She had experienced all the family stress that Jeff had gone through and now she had this exciting, if not stressful, news to share.

Their three children had been on a mission that day to create as much noise as they possibly could. Their living room looked like New York City after a ticker tape parade for a championship team. At one point, while she was on a conference call, the noise was so loud that she was certain her children had sneaked in a heavy metal rock band and had facilitated a concert for the neighborhood children.

Kate's stress level was high.

Jeff's stress level was high.

Neither had done anything to contribute to the other person's stress. And yet, they were sitting on the brink of a proverbial nuclear war.

When Jeff walked in the door, they began a dance that would lead them to one of the biggest fights in their twelve years of marriage. Jeff said hi and leaned in for a short kiss. Kate was distracted. He took that to mean she was upset with him and the monster in his head began spinning a tale about how she had to be mad at him and somehow he did something that she was ready to rip him apart over. He was a failure. One more person to tell him how he was screwing up. Please note: she didn't say any of this, but he heard it in his head just the same.

Kate saw his body language tense up and figured he was probably mad at her because of something her parents had said last week. She secretly felt like she was constantly failing at this parenting thing and probably the spouse thing too.

About ninety minutes later, the start that ignited the gas leak was struck.

Boom went the house. House pets ran for cover. Children cried. In the end, they both cried. Tears of joy streamed down their cheeks next to red-hot tears of lament.

Deep wounds lacerated each soul and scabbed over.

When the fight was over, neither person could remember what set it off or why it had been so intense. They couldn't remember why it had burned like a prairie fire through their hearts and souls. They had failed to recognize the rising escalation and to work at de-escalating it to a manageable place. As the stress poured in, they allowed the pressure to increase. As it increased, they stopped trying to tolerate the stress, because they wanted it to stop. This is an important distinction. Tolerating stress is not the same as trying to make it stop.

When couples are tempted to make the stress stop, they aren't really interested in solving the problem as much as they want to make the discomfort go away. When that becomes their goal, it can become all-consuming. Like a diver starved for oxygen desperately kicking for the surface and clean air, you may focus on how to make the discomfort stop. This will often cause you to bulldoze your partner as though he were a hollow and rotted-out tree, leaving devastation and destruction in your wake.

When we are in this state, we are solving the wrong problem: how to make the discomfort stop rather than move the relationship forward.

I once heard a story about a couple who was traveling with their two college-age sons. They had a plan that the wife would call a pizza place approximately forty-five minutes down the road from where they were leaving. They had spent a wonderful day watching their oldest son play in a bowl game. The plan also called for the wife to give the directions from the cellphone.

The husband was the driver. He saw the team busses start to pull out before they were ready. He didn't want to get stuck behind a long line of busses navigating the crazy Florida roads. So, he pulled out before the pizza was ordered. Because the pizza wasn't ordered, the wife needed to use her phone to both give directions and order the pizza. Her phone lacked those capabilities.

Her frustration level skyrocketed.

The husband began to experience frustration because he knew he had a turn coming up, but he didn't know where it was for certain.

"Do I take this exit?"

"Um, uh, maybe… hold on, I'm on the phone with the pizza place."

"Well, the pizza won't matter if we miss the exit. Hang up!"

Stress went high.

Words were exchanged.

Later, as they processed the fight, they realized that most of the fight was about frustration that had nothing to do with each other. Once the fire had burned out and they looked at the mess they had, they realized it was a fire they created. They saw the stress in each other and failed to tolerate it. It increased painful discomfort for them, and that fire raged.

Once the stress escalated, they were unable to de-escalate themselves in any way. The less they could tolerate the stress, the more they escalated. Their number-one goal was to stop being uncomfortable. They didn't want the other person to be angry with them.

This is the most common reason I hear for people avoiding engaging in uncomfortable talks. They stay out of the circle of conflict because the other person might get mad at them.

Imagine going to the emergency room knowing your leg is broken, but the doctor tells you he's going to let it stay broken and eventually it will heal. She doesn't want you to feel pain.

Your leg would "heal."

Eventually, you could probably walk on it again. But it wouldn't heal. You'd have a limp. The doctor would not be doing you any favors. In fact, she would be harming you.

We do this same type of harm to our relationships when we refuse to engage in the uncomfortable emotions of our relationships.

This does not mean that we should engage the conflict immediately. Sometimes, de-escalating means taking time to cool down. Giving yourself time to de-escalate is a prerequisite for tolerating the stress that comes with the emotional conflict that is part of merging two lives into one.

It's okay to take some time away. It's not okay to take time away and never get back to the issue.

Tolerating the stress means that you will force yourself to engage the stress. It does not go away if you do not engage it. It acts more like a raging fire that dies down but still smolders. Like the dormant fire, our emotions smoke beneath the surface, crackling. Waiting for a gulp of fresh oxygen—oxygen that looks like another potential fight.

Once we've found a way to de-escalate enough to tolerate the stress of engaging in the uncomfortable emotions of discussing the disagreement, we have to problem solve.

Too often, couples try to problem solve while they are escalated. They also lack the skills necessary to work through the issue. This creates its own level of stress. That's part of the reason this book exists and I do what I do: to give couples the skills necessary to problem solve in a constructive manner.

The next section of the book will deal with those skills.

Chapter 14:

What Is Communication?

Almost every couple I meet tells me that their biggest problem is improving their communication. So, I ask them, "What is communication?"

Two things have emerged. One, I rarely get a cogent, complete answer. Most of the time, I get a lot of, "Well, you know… it's talking." At this point, their partner will usually jump in with a clarification that takes the entire conversation in a different direction. This brings me to the second thing that often happens: couples disagree on what it means to communicate.

Which brings me to next question for them and for you. If two people don't agree on what it means to communicate, how can they accomplish communication?

Take a break from reading for a moment and text your three closest friends. Ask them to define communication and see if you agree with their answers. If you do, that's great; if not, allow me to offer you a three-part definition.

Communication is the words we use, plus emotion, plus the story created in our minds.

So often, I hear couples argue over the words used, when in reality, they disagree over the story of what those words mean. They hunker down and dissect what was said and assume they know what was meant, but they rarely ask about the emotions behind the other person's reaction. The argument runs for needless hours because the couple fails to find common ground around these three points. Let's look at each component for a moment.

The Words We Use

Too many arguments end up going in circles around the words that people used. How many times have you heard a couple argue over what was said?

"You said blue."

"No! I said azure."

My example is a little far-fetched, but not too far. This destroys emotional security because we often fail to accurately remember what was said. By arguing about the words used, we never get to the emotion and especially to the "story in our head" part. Without those parts, we'll never get to understand the meaning or have true communication. This is important to remember because we often argue of the validity of the lens each person used in the conversation.

We want to find some point of agreement on the words, especially when that agreement is necessary to move forward. For instance, if you said that you would be at the restaurant at 6:30, but your partner thought you said 7:00, you are probably not going to find agreement on what was said. For whatever reason, you both had a different recollection of what happened. Arguing over what was said is only going to lead to your participating in a continuous circle of disagreement.

But, if you can come to an agreement on how you both can better communicate the next time, you will find a more productive time. Of course, you will first have to decide if this has to be a problem or not.

The words only matter if they stop us from moving forward. Now, I know what you're thinking: "But, Joe, words have meaning and consequences."

I agree.

That's why I'm suggesting you focus on doing something that improves that meaning by focusing on how to ensure you are both on the same page next time. Without that focus, the meaning of the words will never actually matter.

You might be wondering if there is a time when the words actually matter. Yes, if hurtful words are used, it is important to pursue that conversation until agreement can be made.

A number of years ago in my own marriage, my

wife expressed frustration when I would say, "I have to go," when it was time to hang up the phone. We live in a rural bedroom community thirty minutes from the city where I was going to graduate school and I had at least a one-hour commute each day. As a result, we spent a lot of time talking on the phone (don't worry, I was hands-free before it was cool). As we would approach the end of the conversation, I would often end it with, "I have to go."

My wife doesn't like those words. It doesn't matter that her dislike for them makes no sense to me. What matters is that she doesn't like them. So I asked her what she would want me to say when I was ready to hang up. She told me that I could say, "Okay, honey..." or something like that.

I asked her, "So if I say, 'Okay, honey...' you'll know that means I have to go?" Her affirmative response was almost immediate.

In this case, the words I used very much mattered and there was an easy fix to crafting them in a way that allowed my wife to feel heard, valued, and safe.

Often, couples put a lot of effort into arguing over the words they or their partner used when that isn't *really* what they're arguing about. What they really disagree about is the meaning of those words or the story that those words are spinning in their heads. The challenge they face is their emotions clouding their ability to express that meaning. This exacerbates their ability to clearly explain the story running through their heads.

THE EMOTIONS BEHIND THOSE WORDS

If I said to you, "Hey, Beavis!" would you feel that was a term of endearment? No, why not? Would it evoke positive emotions in your heart? For years in my house growing up, that was a term of endearment that somehow my brother started and my mom picked up. To this day, my sister will occasionally throw it into a Snapchat or text to me.

The story that phrase spins out in my head is probably different from the story it spins out in your head. Why?

Because we have different interpretations and emotions around the phrase. The words we use are rarely free from emotional interpretation. This is why it is so dangerous to argue through text messages. Tone in such things is often affected by the reader's emotional state and interpretation of the writer's emotions.

Emotions that attach themselves to words are a filter to our understanding. How many times have you thought someone was mad or angry when they weren't? How many times have you ever had someone think you were mad or angry when you weren't?

This emotional lens acts as a filter for the words we hear. It shapes them into meaning. For instance, the use of Beavis as a term of endearment came from the family mocking a TV show that to my knowledge no one in our family actually watched. To this day, when I see anything related to that show, I feel a measure of happy emotions. The story it spins in my head and the emotions I experience are so tightly interwoven that I can have a hard time distinguishing between them. Where does one start and the other end?

To be honest, I'm not sure. I do know that emotions filter what we hear and help to give it meaning.

There are some tricky aspects to this, though, that we have to navigate with skill and precision if we're going to become skilled word ninjas. I often tell my clients that I want them to become word ninjas. A ninja was someone who developed a very specific set of skills to protect others and those things he valued greatly. That is the level of skill I want us to develop for our partner with our words.

We have to develop the ability to parse out our own emotions and what we think are the emotions of our partner. An area where I often find a lot of pushback when it comes to emotions is in the area of anger.

JON AND AMY

Jon and Amy came in one day for their weekly session. They had been coming to see me for a little over three months. Jon was a gifted stand-up comedian while Amy was a gifted surgeon. Amy was obviously distressed. I start almost every session the same way. I ask two questions.

How was the week?

Is there anything you would like to make sure we talk about this week?

Amy began immediately: "He got angry!"

To which I replied, "Okay…" I was hoping she was going to tell me more about the interaction.

"I mean, he got *really* angry! His face was red. His ears looked like someone painted them with a purple paintbrush!"

"What did he do?" I asked.

"Do! What did he do? He was angry!" Her faced pleaded with me to hear her. She couldn't believe I didn't understand why Jon getting angry was bad.

"He was angry because I didn't book the reservation for the dog kennel when he thought I should have."

At this point, Jon jumped in with an excited, "That's not true. I was frustrated because you said you were going to do it and you didn't. Then the place filled up—"

"Oh! So it's okay for you to get angry and belligerent!" This was the first time in the fifteen-minute exchange that my ears actually perked up. The word *belligerent* implied action.

"I wasn't belligerent. I didn't even say anything other than one word!"

Before this argument could continue down a path to fruitlessness, I asked Amy if she agreed with Jon that he only said one word. She did. I asked her what one word he used. She looked at me with almost glee, believing now that I would finally see her side of this sordid affair.

"He said, 'Okay!'" Her facial expression clearly stated, "Can you believe it?"

As I pulled the sleeves of my favorite hoodie down toward my wrist to buy a little bit of time, I asked her why this word was bad.

"Because he was angry!" When pressed about the word itself, she agreed that in and of itself, it had no value one way or the other. It conveys no real meaning alone. But, because he was angry and she knew he was angry, it spun a story in her head that he was dismissing her or talking down to her.

"What if I told you that I think anger is just a chemical reaction in the body and it doesn't really mean much?" I wanted to say more, but I was unable to do so because my question elicited a loud groan and a *humph* from her as she glared at me as though I was a Tolkien brute that barely understood English.

"He. Was. Angry!" She pronounced each word with an emphatic pause as though she were verbally poking me in the chest.

"But so what? What does it matter that he was angry?" I pushed back over the beginning of a protest by Jon. You see, he wanted to argue with her about whether or not he was angry. When in reality, what mattered was what she thought that emotion meant and what he thought it didn't mean. In fact, I offered to role-play their argument for them. Jon would say he wasn't angry but was actually frustrated and disappointed.

Amy would respond with something along the lines of contempt because she knew he was angry or she might acquiesce with a "fine, you were *frustrated*," putting a heavy emphasis on the word *frustrated*. Then he would justify his reasons for being frustrated and she would push back against him being angry again and wonder (often out loud) why he couldn't just admit he was angry.

The whole time they would miss the point that it was Amy's internal dialogue about what his anger meant that started this spinning orb of a fight.

"What do you mean it doesn't matter?" she asked. "Are you suggesting that it's okay to be angry?"

"Yes, that's exactly what I'm suggesting," I replied. At this point, I had their attention.

"I think anger is nothing more than a chemical reaction most of the time. It's not the anger that matters; it's what we do with it that matters. When a person gets angry, what really matters is what they do with their words and actions. Certainly, if a person is walking around getting angry a lot over things, that could be an indication of a problem; but for the most part, I think anger isn't a whole lot different than hunger or sexual attraction or any other chemical reaction in our body."

At this point, you might be reacting much like Amy did with more than a little bit of incredulity. But how is it any different? It's just an emotion. One that we often do terrible things with, but even that sentence supports my position. It's not the anger; it's the terrible things that are done with it. Those are actions.

Actions have value. Emotions are experienced. They happen. What we do with them is what matters.

But if we have a position that certain emotions are bad, we will constantly spin the presence of that emotion out to a negative story when it presents itself in our intimate partner. This expectation will often cause us to see the negative action in our partner even if it actually isn't there. This can lead to a mindset that growth must be immediate or it is a failure.

WORDS + EMOTION + STORY

Whatever is said only has meaning because of interpretations. The accuracy of that interpretation is vital to a healthy conversation. Couples often take the words they hear and couple the emotions they believe both parties are feeling and interpret that into meaning. This becomes the story spinning in one's head.

In every conversation, there are a number of conversations happening. There is what the speaker thinks they are saying and what they are actually saying. There is what the listener thinks they are hearing and what they are actually hearing. These two things are not always the same. There is dialogue running in each person's head about what needs to get done later today and the stressors of life.

Behind these conversations is a babbling brook that never stops running. In fact, for most people, it is nothing more than white noise. But it is a powerful white noise that drives the person's understanding of their own self, their self-worth, and I believe, their view of the rest of the world. This babbling brook is constantly whispering to each person.

It says things such as, "You are not enough... You're too fat, too short, too tall, too skinny..." Like a poison, it often slinks its way into our system undetected, spewing hatred and death. This brook becomes the primary filter for our path to understanding the meaning of what is happening in a conversation.

For most guys, the brook just keeps whispering, "You're screwing up, and you'll never be enough. You'll always be a screw-up," and other discouraging thoughts. This is why when a man's partner brings up something he could do better, all he hears is, "I'm screwing up again."

For most women, the message is that they are not desirable. No one will actually be willing to fight to be with them and pursue them and wrestle with whatever it takes to get to know them—truly get to know their deepest inner thoughts and desires. So when her partner reacts with anger to a suggestion on how something could be done better, she sees it as a reaction to her because her brook is telling her she's not worthy. Perhaps this is why the phrase "You are enough" seems to be so ubiquitous.

Go back to Amy and Jon for a moment. Was she really upset that he was angry or did she interpret his anger through her own brook of inadequacy? Was she already feeling shame because she should have called the kennel but put it off until it was too late? Did she hear one of her parents scolding eleven-year-old her for putting off something that they felt she should have been doing? My guess is that much, if not all, of that is true. She interpreted Jon's anger as a rejection of her. Even if he was just angry or frustrated about the loss of the kennel reservation.

Brené Brown puts it this way in her book"

When I talk to couples, I can see how shame creates one of the most lethal dangers to a relationship. Women, who feel shame when they don't feel heard or validated, often resort to pushing and provoking with criticism ("Why don't you ever do enough?" or "You never get it right"). Men, in turn, who feel shame when they feel criticized for being inadequate, either shut down (leading women to poke and provoke more) or come back with anger.[1]

Where does that shame come from? It comes from our personal brook and the interpretation we shape with it. When I can convince couples that anger is nothing more than a chemical reaction and what we do matters more than what we feel, they begin to move on and heal. The anger is still there, at first. In fact, it still bubbles up; but over time, as the person starts to focus on appropriate behavior both internally and externally,

---

1 Brené Brown, *Daring Greatly: How the Courage to Be Vulnerable Transforms the Way We Live, Love, Parent, and Lead.* New York: Penguin Publishing Group, page 103.

it starts to dissipate. It goes away.

Let's play out the rest of the conversation with Jon and Amy.

"Amy, could you tell me what you were feeling when you realized that the kennel wasn't going to have space for your dogs?"

"I felt panic. I knew Jon was going to be mad. I was worried we were going to have to use that old kennel that we used and hated before, or worse, we'd have to change our travel plans. We've been working so hard and planning this trip for so long. I just felt... *ugh*."

Tears pooled in her eyes as she continued, "I was certain that I had ruined our time away."

At this point, Jon reached out and tentatively touched her knee, concern in his eyes. For the first time in this exchange, he was able to pass the eyeball test. The eyeball test in counseling is different than what it might mean in other circles. The eyeball test is the ability to take our eyes out of our own head and put them in our partner's head so that we can see the incident we're experiencing through their lens. This skill is often called *empathy*.

"Jon, can you tell me what you were feeling when Amy told you the reservation couldn't be made?"

Jon swallowed and took a sip of his coffee as he pondered his answer. His words came out in staccato bursts. "I... felt... frustrated... because I thought..."

Before he could finish, Amy began to interrupt with large teardrops falling down her face. "I knew you were mad at me. I didn't mean to…"

Before she could finish (we talked the next week about the importance of allowing our partner to finish their sentences), Jon interrupted her.

"I wasn't angry or even frustrated *at you!*" He put special emphasis and body inflection on the last two words. "I was frustrated because I had all the same concerns that you had about Seashell (their dog) and that terrible kennel from before. I was also worried that our trip was going to have to be canceled. I feel like we've been making some great progress and I was afraid that this trip that I've been so looking forward to wasn't going to happen."

For the moment, I wasn't in the room with them anymore. They were just two people in love, trying to navigate the issues of life. Sadly, I had to interrupt this moment with a few more questions. It was a counseling session, after all.

"Perfect. Now, Jon, could you tell me what you were feeling when you felt Amy's frustration that you were angry?"

"I wasn't angry."

"I know, you were frustrated. Either way, do you think you could articulate what you were feeling when she said you were angry?"

"I felt like she was accusing me of something that wasn't true. I felt like she was saying I was like my dad. I didn't know what she wanted me to do. I followed those rules you gave us, and she still got mad. (We'll get to those rules he referenced in the next chapter). Somehow, some way, I was failing."

"Is it safe to say that you didn't see a 'win' in this situation?"

"Yes, that's exactly it. I had no idea which way to go."

"How did you react to that?"

"I shut down. That's the way I often react when I don't know what to do."

"Wait. You thought I was judging you?" Amy's tone was full of incredulity.

Jon laughed a short, nervous laugh. "Well, yeah. I had no way to calm you down."

At this point, I asked Jon why it was so important to calm her down, as he had put it.

"Well, I didn't want to fight with her. I mean, I was disappointed and a little nervous about what it meant for our plans, but I wasn't interested in fighting with her. I didn't want the whole trip ruined."

Notice that they both spun out the interaction in their heads to almost the same story. Both of them saw the other person's negative or dark emotions as a bad thing that had to be eliminated. They were both afraid of failing and of the fight that they believed would stem from their fight. And yet, they both reacted in such a way to push the relationship toward a fight.

Amy did this almost immediately, while Jon tried a few different strategies before resorting back to what he was comfortable with, even though he knew from past experience that those actions wouldn't get him the result he was looking to achieve.

One of the most common stress points between couples is the question regarding how one presents their true emotions in a relationship without causing grief. Almost all couples counselors hear from their clients that they need to improve communication.

When I ask them to define better communication, they look at me confused, as though the definition should be as plain as the paint on my wall. I tell them a little secret: I don't think they need better communication. They need communication that actually leads to intimacy and builds friendship.

Most couples do a decent job at communicating. Of course, they can do better, but that is not what their relationship needs. It needs intimacy and their current communication pattern actually blows that intimacy up.

Wait!

You might be thinking, "Aren't you then saying that they do need better communication?" No, I'm saying they need a better goal. And better communication is the means to that goal.

It starts with how we enter the conversation.

Most of the time, we enter a conversation like a wrecking ball unleashed on a building, somehow expecting that it will build a beautiful structure instead of doing what it is designed to do: destroy the old. We start out making accusations and statements of fact about things we think. We take a barrel of jet fuel and drop a box of lit fireworks in it and wonder why it exploded.

In my experience, most couples will convey meaning to each other. This is what we typically mean when we say the word *communication*. So when you are mad at someone, telling him or her that you are mad is communicating. Interestingly enough, what people usually mean when they say that they need to get better at communication is two things:

1. How do I communicate so the other person doesn't get mad?

2. How do I communicate so the person understands, because they obviously don't understand me or they wouldn't be mad right now.

Sometimes, I have to try hard not to chuckle at that last one. Usually, I think they understood the person just fine. Their reaction was just different than expected.

Instead, I like to ask three questions to help us form a good lead into an emotional conversation. First of all, how do we enter into the circle of conflict without setting fire to each other? That is to say, what is the best possible way for me to share the facts as I understand them, and my emotions about what happened without leaving scars in you? Second, how do we stay engaged in this conversation long enough to solve it without leaving scars? This is one of the reasons I think most couples just give up on their fights. They don't know how to solve the conflict so they just scrap the whole conversation. Everyone is still bleeding, but the conversation has died. The third and last question is: how do we exit the circle of conflict and re-enter into "normal" life in a better way? Can we have this conflict and not walk around for days with this cloud of relationship decay and death hanging over our heads? I believe the answer is yes, and it starts with how you enter into the conversation.

In the next chapter, we are going to cover strategies and techniques that will help Jon, Amy, and you to better understand the story running from each person's brook and how to better communicate in face of its emotional onslaught.

Chapter 15:

Utilizing the ABCs of Good Communication

Y OU MAY REMEMBER THAT ONE OF OUR QUESTIONS about conflict was how to engage it without causing unnecessary pain. One of the best possible ways to enter into conflict is to begin with the facts as you understand them and your feelings about those facts. There should be no, "You made me…" or "It made me…" statements. Simply facts and "I felt."

"When you start swearing at me, I feel disrespected" is the best way to begin the conversation. I call this the ABC or This/That Method of communication. "When **A** is said or done, I feel **B** and I'd like to feel **C**." We do not always need to state letter C—sometimes it is obvious. That is why you will sometimes hear me call this this the This/That Method where *this* and *that* replace **A** and **B**.

"When **this** happens, I feel **that**."

Obvious, right? But let me ask a question. When

was the last time you had a conversation that allowed you to take ownership of your own feelings? This method allows your partner to take ownership for their actions while you take ownership for your feelings. It allows both people to interact like adults who are on the same team moving toward the same goal.

This allows the conversation to open in a safe way. It invites rather than insults. The topics will still often be heavy. You will still feel your heart race to the top of your throat (let's be honest: there's a decent chance that your partner will be tempted to react defensively until he learns a new response), but if you use this method, you are moving toward the goal of safe entry into conversations about conflict.

Let's look at an example.

JERRY AND LUCY

Let's go back to Jerry and Lucy for a moment. You might remember them from the chapter on expectations. When we last visited them, Jerry was just about to ask his wife about why she had chosen a route to the beach.

"So I'm wondering why you are going this way."

She sighed a deep, soul-shattering sigh of annoyance. Here was his opportunity to use the ABC Method of communicating.

"When you sigh like that, I feel like you're annoyed at me and that you don't want me to ask you any questions about what you do."

She looked over at him and told him he was right.

"I don't see why I have to answer to you on what route I chose. It's our off day—what does it matter which route I choose?"

"So you feel like I'm interrogating because I asked about the route?"

"Yes, when you ask me questions about things that don't matter, I feel like you want to control what's going on. I'm driving. It's my choice and I like this route better than the one you take. I don't agree that your way is quicker most of the time and I think this one is more scenic. I wish you could just enjoy the drive with me. "

Lucy did a great job here of expressing to him how she felt about what happened and what she believed about him. He is under no obligation to agree with her, but they are well on the path to good communication. Notice how she followed the pattern of ABC.

- When **A** happens,
- "When you ask me questions about things that don't matter…"
- I feel **B**.
- "I feel like you want to control what's going…"
- I would like to feel **C**.
- "I wish you could just enjoy the drive with me."

It's important to note that their conversation isn't over. They have done a good job of overcoming negative emotions to start a healthy dialogue.

The ABC Method answers our first question about conflict: "How do we enter into conflict without hurting each other?" Jerry and Lucy can continue using this skill to further their conversation.

Jerry could tell her he was just trying to talk to her. He could ask her if there was a way he could ask her that question without her feeling like he was trying to control her. One of the greatest advantages of using the ABC Method is that it creates multiple avenues of understanding that can be pursued.

Using the ABC or This/That Method to begin potentially dangerous conversations sets a couple up for success by choosing the least threatening opening. It simply states facts. What happened? What was said? What was done? What feelings were experienced? These are key aspects to healthy interactions.

It's important to note that the conversation should only deal in facts. The facts may be debated at some level. In other words, both parties may not agree with everything that happened or on what was said, but they should be making an active attempt to deal with only things that happened or were experienced. Both people need to be able to express the facts as they understand them.

By doing this, they create an opportunity to understand how both sides experienced the interaction. Understanding is the first step in the journey forward toward health. In the illustration above, Jerry and Lori still have not dealt with Jerry's feeling that Lori was annoyed or his fear that they would get caught in a cycle of fights. He could use this method to broach that subject. It would sound something like the following conversation:

"I wasn't sure what to bring up. I feel like we've been fighting a lot lately and I'm afraid that we're going to fight today. I'm afraid that our constant fighting is a sign that we are growing apart and that our relationship is in trouble."

Utilizing the Mirror Method, which we will talk about in the next chapter, will help the conversation move forward from this opening dance.

Instead of saying, "You are lying," a person using the ABC Method might say, "When you tell me one thing and my eyes see something else, I feel like I don't have the whole story."

It avoids all of the emotional hazards because it focuses only on what's happened without shifting blame. It doesn't escalate the situation by utilizing hunting or running. It's obvious when this is happening that sitting out is not occurring.

Chapter 16:

The Mirror Method

THE MIRROR METHOD WILL ALLOW YOU TO HAVE A conversation with your loved one in a healthy way, no matter how emotionally charged the topic. This skill creates prime conditions for emotional security to grow. Utilizing the Mirror Method is attempting to communicate to the other person that you hear and value them and that you are safe for them. When done correctly, this method will allow you to answer all three questions (Am I safe, heard, and valued?) without attacking your spouse. Think of it as allowing the storm to blow itself out before you dive into repairing the boat.

There are two distinct ways to use the Mirror Method. The first way is the long way. Look at this way as the driver's education method of two hands on the wheel at all times. Do you remember when you first started driving? Did everything seem so fast and out of control? Now, how often do you have two hands on the wheel?

THE LONG WAY

In the Mirror Method, we want to work through four steps. They are:
1. Listen
2. Affirm
3. Repeat/Reword
4. Confirm

The first thing you need to do is *listen*. This sounds so simple, but remember we want to do this when we are completely stressed with the person. When is it harder to listen than when you are in the middle of a fight? You want to speak. You want to defend your own honor. You want the other person to shut up so you can talk. Listening means that you really seek to hear what is being said. You must strive to hear not just the words they are saying but also the intent behind those words.

The second thing you want to do is *affirm* the person's value to you. You must affirm the importance of the relationship and how much you want to work on it. You confess that you don't currently understand and state that you want to hear what the person is saying, and that you desire to understand how they are feeling. You want to hear their emotions underneath what is going on.

The third thing you want to do is *repeat/reword*

what your spouse is saying. This lets them know you are really trying to hear them—that you are listening. By not adding your own editorial to it, you are communicating that you don't want to fix them, but you do want to have a healthy relationship and are willing to repair that if necessary.

The fourth thing you want to do is *confirm* that what you think you heard and understood the other person communicate. We end this portion with the all-important question, "Is that right?"

When you put these four steps together, it might look something like this:

"I'm sorry we're not communicating very well right now. Our relationship is important to me. You are important to me. I want to understand what you are saying better. Would it be all right with you if I repeated what I think you're saying and what I think you mean?"

At this point, you would wait for them to say yes, and then you would state to them what it is you think they are saying and ask them if that is right.

THE SHORT WAY

In the short way, you simply state what they said to you. You might say, "So you're saying…" or "What I hear you saying is…" or any version of this opening, which can lead you to repeat what they're saying. In the beginning, that is all that matters: saying to them what they are saying to you so they know you're hearing them. This allows you to begin the process of moving away from the hurt and pain of whatever is wrong and causing stress toward healing and wholeness.

Relationships will always have stress and disagreements, but we need better ways to process those disagreements and that stress. This is the first step in a brand-new world of communication. When you become good at this skill, you can process any disagreement.

I talked to a couple recently who went an entire calendar year without a major fight. They had disagreements (some major disagreements), but they didn't have fights that left wounds and scars. They actually had disagreements that lasted days, but they didn't turn to fights where hurtful words were used to gain leverage.

This method allows you to engage in really passionate disagreements and still talk in a way that allows each person to be heard. It allows the pressure of the conflict to be managed so that healing can occur. When you use this method, your partner knows you're trying to hear them. This automatically moves the anger meter down a few degrees. This is not a problem solver, but it is a tool to help *you* be the problem solver.

KEVIN AND JENNI

Kevin and Jenni came to see me about their marriage. They had been married for almost ten years and felt as if they weren't communicating very well. Jenni felt like Kevin never listened to her. After a few minutes in the session with them, it was hard for me to disagree with her. He would interrupt her and finish her thoughts. He would often tell her what "she really meant." It was easy to watch them float through the dangerous conversations of emotional hazards fairly quickly.

When I pointed out to Kevin that I could see Jenni's point of view, I asked him if he saw it. He said that he did, but he didn't know how to change it. I taught him the Mirror Method. The conversation looked something like this:

Kevin: Jenni, I love you. I'm really sorry we're not communicating all that well right now. I want to understand what you are saying and what you are trying to tell me by what you are saying. Would it be all right with you if I repeated to you what I think you're saying and what you're trying to tell me?

Jenni: I don't see how it will matter, but sure, go ahead. You never actually listen anyhow.

Kevin: I think you're saying that I never actually let you finish your sentences and that I don't listen to you at all. You feel like I'm dismissing your feelings and thoughts because of this. Is that right?

Jenni: Darn tootin'! You always just cut me off and you never actually let me say anything.

At this point, Jenni went back into repeating everything she had just said to Kevin. Her level of resentment with Kevin meant that she wanted to make sure he got the point that she was hurt. He looked at me with a "See, I told you so" look on his face. I was actually pretty happy. This was working exactly like it should. I instructed him to go back to mirroring her again.

Kevin: Jenni, I'm glad you feel that I am starting to hear you and better understand you. Would you mind if I repeated to you what I think you said that time?

Jenni: I don't care.

Kevin: You're saying that I cut you off and that I don't listen. This hurts your feelings? Is that right?

At this point, Jenni's entire demeanor changed. For the first time, she seemed to feel heard. Of course, this leaves the biggest question to just hang in the air: Now what?

Now, it is really important for Kevin to ask one simple question: what he can do differently next time or offer an option for what he will do differently next time. He could say something like this:

I am sorry that I've been doing this to you. I'm going to be on the lookout for it whenever we talk and try not to do it. If I do it, would you be willing to tell me that I am cutting you off? Would you be willing to remind that I asked you to tell me and ask me to stop?

He's not trying to tell her why she's wrong. He's not trying to fix her. He's simply trying to fix the problem that is hurting their marriage. He realizes that it doesn't matter what he thinks he's communicating.

The only thing that really matters is what *she* thinks he's communicating. This is revolutionary for most marriages. Just listening at a heart level can bring so much healing to those we love.

KEVIN AND JENNI: THE SHORT WAY

To implement the Mirror Method the short way is to simply streamline it is a little bit. For most couples, they can get by with just starting at the reword/repeat version of the story. It might look like this:

Kevin: So you're saying that I don't let you finish your sentences and that you feel like I'm dismissing your emotions?

Jenni: Yes, you also won't let me—

Kevin: Well, that's because I—

Jenni: See, you're doing it right there!

Kevin: Oh! Holy cow, I've never noticed that before.

At this point, it would be very appropriate for Kevin to then ask what he can do differently or attempt to offer his own alternative way forward.

When people practice this, they tend to get hung up on the idea of how to start. People tell me some common things tend to hang them up when they are attempting the Mirror Method. First, they tell me they want to argue with what the person is saying to them. They tell me that their emotions get so riled up that the idea of being a better listener doesn't enter their brain. To be successful, they will need to be able to suppress that feeling and do what is best for the relationship.

The second tripping point I hear is that they feel stupid trying to say what has been just said to them. They wonder if the other person will just get angrier because they are repeating to them what was said instead of offering an argument. Will this method really allow them to engage in conflict in a way that works?

Occasionally, someone tells me they don't know what to say when they are trying this method. They either feel that they are overwhelmed or just a slow processor of what is being said. "I'm not that quick on my feet" is a common phrase I hear. I'd like to take a moment to answer these three common concerns.

WHEN YOU WANT TO ARGUE

The simple answer here would be not to engage that feeling. We tend to feel that we have to do what we feel like doing. As if somehow we are slaves to our feelings, but simple logic disproves this notion. How often do you really want to go to work? I'm certain the answer is not 100 percent of the time, yet I bet you show up far more often than you want to be there.

In other words, we control our feelings all the time. Simply because you are tempted to fight with your spouse regarding what they are saying doesn't mean you have to argue with them. Just because you want to talk over them doesn't mean you have to talk over them. It simply means that you want to do that. You can choose to engage in the Mirror Method in order to help your spouse feel more heard and understood. This is a matter of choice, not a matter of slavery.

WHEN YOU FEEL STUPID

As human beings, we have a great fear of feeling inadequate. We are all insecure about many things and in desperate need of affirmation. Many times, our fights are driven by our feelings of inadequacy as they are fed by our own feelings of guilt, shame, and fear. Any possibility of deeper understanding and resolution can be lost before we ever get started when we let those themes run our decisions.

When you feel stupid, it does not actually mean anything besides the fact that you feel that way. Most of the time, I have found that one's partner respects the fact that he or she is trying to play the game. Almost everyone recognizes that this skill is hard and that it is not the normal way we have all learned to communicate. The best thing to do when this feeling hits us is to start basic. Push through the fear by saying the most basic thing you can say.

WHEN YOU DON'T KNOW WHAT TO SAY

Keep it simple. Don't make it too complicated. Pick something he said and ask if that's what he's saying.

The point is that you're seeking to better understand your partner. You are attempting to find the emotions behind the words that he or she is using. It doesn't have to be complicated. If the statement is, "You're always telling me that you'll be home by seven and you never get home before eight!" you might consider some of the following to mirror to them.

What is the emotion that is driving this statement? How might this be restated for better understanding? The response might be, "You're upset because I'm not getting home when I say I am?" This sounds so simple, and it seems that it might actually make things worse, but the truth is that it almost always makes things better. It tells the other person that you are more interested in listening than you are in fighting.

Your partner knows you want to argue. They know the first instinct is to defend, dismiss, or discount what she is saying. When you engage her by obviously seeking to better understand what exactly it is that she's communicating, you are telling her by your actions how much you actually love her. Remember, how many people actually feel heard in their life? When you begin by seeking to hear and understand, you begin to build trust and respect.

Moving beyond Simply Restating

The point of the Mirror Method is not to simply restate what your partner is saying to you but to understand the emotions and feelings that are driving it. You want to know if there is something you can change. You want to know what is happening with him or her on an emotional level. What is causing your partner grief and stress? You want to understand the triggers. This is important because it allows you to plan for the future and it creates an opportunity for the real problem to be resolved. As I've previously written, most of our arguments never actually deal with the trigger or problem that caused the issue.

WHAT HAPPENS WHEN THE PROBLEM IS SOMETHING THAT CANNOT BE CHANGED?

When you encounter a problem that cannot be changed, you need to look at the problem differently. Remember the goal of mirroring is creating a situation where the other person feels heard, not necessarily getting your way. When you encounter something you don't think can be changed, you need to answer some questions.

1. What do I want?

This probably seems somewhat silly, but I cannot tell you how many times I have worked with people and asked them, "What do you want?" only to hear sputters about what they *don't* want or what the other person *isn't* doing. You need to make this as simple and concise as possible. Ideally, you should be able to say in a sentence or two what you want out of the situation.

2. What does my partner want?

Again, this sounds so simple, but I can tell you from experience, it is rarely as simple as it sounds. We often think we know what the other person wants, but in reality, we have no idea. Again, you want this to break down to the simplest form possible. Can you, in one or two sentences, explain what your partner wants in this situation? Can you answer what would have to be true for him or her to feel as though they have "won" in this situation?

3. Is it possible for both partners to get what they want?

4. What are possible compromises?

KYLE AND JULIE

Kyle and Julie had been struggling with money. Kyle was in the middle of a career change after failing at his own business a little over a year ago. He went back to school and worked at a job he believed was menial. Julie had her own issues: she was struggling with insecurity and was the casualty of her parents going through a nasty divorce. Her father was caught cheating on her mother after twenty-eight years of marriage. Kyle just came home later than he had told Julie he would be home. She was frustrated because she expected him home over an hour and a half ago. He was frustrated because he couldn't find a part at the junkyard to fix his car and was afraid he will not have the money to fix it.

Let's look in on the conversation between them.

Julie: Where have you been?

Kyle: I've been all around town looking for the stupid part for the car.

Julie: Your phone isn't working?

Kyle: No, it works just fine. Why?

Julie: You said you'd be home over an hour ago! It's almost eight-thirty and you said you would be home by seven! I'm so sick of you—

Kyle: Quit your griping! I don't have to tell you where I am every moment of every day. You're not my mother!

Julie: Oh! You're right, Kyle! I'm just like Karen. Always trying to check up on you to make sure you're going to do what you tell your wife that you're going to do. Forgive me for thinking you might actually be an adult.

Kyle: Don't you blame me. I'd tell you what I'm doing if you weren't always riding me like I'm your third child.

Julie: Maybe I wouldn't treat you like a child if you didn't act like one.

Kyle: Oh! You're right! It's always my fault. It's not like I'm working twelve to fourteen hours a day just trying to keep us afloat here. Maybe if I hadn't lost my job, maybe... a thousand maybes! What do you want from me?

Julie: I want you to...

Notice all of the emotional hazards that they engaged in throughout this conversation. Now let's look at another possible path they could've taken.

Julie: Where have you been?

Kyle: I've been all around town looking for a stupid part for the car.

Julie: Your phone isn't working?

Kyle: No, it works just fine. Why?

Julie: You said you'd be home over an hour ago! It's almost eight-thirty and you said you would be home by seven! I'm so sick of you not taking the time to call me.

Kyle: You're upset because I'm late or...

Julie: No, Kyle, I'm frustrated because you can't seem to take the time to pick up the phone and call me when you're going to be late. It's rude. I would like a phone call from you when you are going to be late.

Notice how she finished with what she wanted. She expressed how she felt about his behavior and she didn't attack him. Also, notice that Kyle sought clarification about why she was upset. He did not assume that he knew the why or how to fix it. He gave her space to express her frustration.

UNDERSTANDING DEFENSIVENESS

Let's consider vigilance and defensiveness. One of our most common defenses to stress is vigilance.

We become "on alert." We navigate through a painful or hurtful situation and then we leave it in a state of vigilance. Likewise, when we recognize a situation that looks similar to a previously painful situation, our defenses kick in and we become vigilant.

The good news is that this is normal and in many situations, it is helpful. The bad news is that it can be destructive in relationships. It can be destructive because this defensiveness becomes an almost involuntary response that causes us not to think in how we respond. We can do things that are destructive to other people that cause us to feel safe. In the end, we're not actually safe, but feeling safe is a powerful aphrodisiac. We have to train ourselves to utilize skills that can keep us safe and keep the person we are interacting with safe. We need to protect and build the relationship.

I have found the illustration of a float to be helpful. Imagine your partner's defensiveness as a float on top of water inside a bucket. If the float goes too high, it will set off explosions and fire. There is no way (that I know of) to engage in most conflicts and not raise defensiveness to some degree. By nature, we are defensive creatures. Almost no one likes being corrected. Almost no one likes being told they need to improve or change.

So we want to choose our words wisely. We want to choose words that allow us to say what needs to be said but move the float up as little as possible. We can start this safe process by being a great listener.

All it takes to be a great listener are time and effort. We have to force ourselves to choose our words wisely. We need to choose to listen instead of speaking. We need to push ourselves to truly hear the person and trust that by being a good listener we will be able to be heard as well. This starts with mirroring. Often, when I work with people who tell me they want to be better at communication, they look at me and say, "Well, that seems simple. I'm sure I'll get it."

Then they don't.

This is more than saying, "I know what you're saying, but…" In fact, if you're leading with that, you don't get what they are saying. At all. The truth is that mirroring is one of the simplest skills you will learn and at the same time, it is one of the hardest skills you will attempt to master. Because it is hard, some people stop.

There is no single better tool that allows you to master your own defensiveness and the defensiveness of those you love than the tool of the Mirror Method. Almost no one feels truly heard and when they do, relationships grow and relational equity skyrockets.

We are actively trying to help our partner feel heard, valued, and safe by employing this one simple technique. Rather than being stuck in the same destructive habits, this method of communicating will allow us to build relational equity and emotional security. As they grow, our relationship will flourish.

Chapter 17:

The Six Rules of Good Communication

(#1-3 of BADFIT)

THERE ARE SIX SIMPLE RULES THAT CAN GUIDE YOU in your conversations with your spouse and those you love. These rules are easy to use but extremely powerful. I have seen them help numerous couples create healthy relationships. Many times, these couples were on the brink of divorce when they began implementing these rules.

They are not a matter of skill or ability. They are simply a matter of choice. Anyone can follow them. When they are followed, our loved ones will feel heard, valued, and safe.

In fact, it's something of a cascading effect. If you are following these simple (but often difficult) rules, you will find that your relationship begins to build momentum toward each person being heard, valued, and safe. These rules keep you from attacking the person. They empower you to discuss deeply emotional and powerful issues without attacking or destroying each other. They allow you to process.

Furthermore, they allow you to find a way to negotiate through your conflict. They tell your partner, "Even though I'm mad, I love you. I want to work this out with you. I want our relationship to be healthy and work in a way that brings us closer together no matter what."

Invariably, when I have worked with couples, those who have embraced these rules have improved their relationship; and the couples who have not embraced them have continued to struggle with their relationship.

These rules can be followed by anyone. They can do everything that I mention above. What they cannot do is simply remove the anger from a person. We need to look at anger like being wet. If someone has water dropped on him, he is still wet regardless of how he reacts. In a similar way, when anger begins coursing through a person's body, it's not going to just stop going through him. It's going to continue. To an extent, people can learn to self-soothe and calm down more quickly over time. Still, the best way to measure a person's growth is based on what they do when they are angry.

Be Intentional—Choosing your actions instead of allowing your actions to choose you

Always avoid always and never say never—Avoiding the traps of sideways conversations

Does it have to be a problem?—Realizing it may not be a problem at all

Facts only—Dealing with what you know versus what you think you know

Issues, not people—Attacking the actions, while building the person up

Today's news—Dealing with the issue in front of you, and staying focused

You only need to remember the acronym: BADFIT. When we fail to follow these six rules in our communication style, we will find that many, if not all, of our relationships will be a "BADFIT" with all apologies to my grammar-minded friends. The best part of these six rules is that they are a choice.

1. Be Intentional

So many people believe they cannot help how they react in a relationship. I will often hear, "I just cannot help it, that is how I feel…" in sessions. I will often agree that that's how they feel. I will quickly challenge the idea that they have to act in a destructive way simply because they're angry or frustrated.

Be intentional about everything you do in your relationship, especially when you are working to build emotional security.

This one seems to be common sense, but so often it is not. So many of us live in a completely reactionary world. We do very little to teach anyone how to regulate their emotions or to help them do the opposite of what their emotions tell them to do.

We almost live as though we are enslaved to our emotions.

We're not slaves. We have to accept two facts when it comes to our choices. We are entirely responsible for our own actions and we cannot blame others. Too often, we choose reactions and then blame our partner for that choice.

A man once told me that he could not help himself when he became angry and that he had to yell at his wife or kids. They simply needed to get on board with the program and everything would be fine. If they would be more agreeable to his plans and do what he wanted them to do, then he wouldn't have to yell at them.

"You have no idea what an emotional fifteen-year-old girl can be like," was one of his favorite quotes.

This idea is hogwash. That is to say, it is as useful as the soapy suds from washing hogs. It has zero value.

Our feelings are a bit of a different animal. We may often experience something that creates an emotional reaction in us that generates intense feelings. These feelings are often like passing showers in the springtime. They are intense with a lot of thunder and lightning, but they are not something we want to utilize in cultivating our crops. In the same way, we cannot use feelings to cultivate ground that is fertile to grow emotional security.

In sessions, I often offer clients a deal. If they can make me yell at them, I will give them a lifetime of free counseling and they can refer someone to me for the same deal. The only stipulation is that they cannot physically touch me. I've never had anyone succeed. I am in control of me. Period.

Almost everyone instinctively knows this truth. Even the guy who tells me he "has to yell at his wife or kids" will often admit that he wants to yell at someone at work but manages to keep the expression of his anger to a minimum. It is the expression of our anger that is often destructive and detrimental to our loved ones. I believe that even in the midst of anger, you can choose to do things that cultivate emotional security. That is the basis for these six rules of communication.

Often, we feel threatened in some way or we feel hurt during an argument or disagreement with a spouse or loved one. Exasperating the moment is the often-false belief that it will always be like this. This being negative, irritating, and painful. At this point, all rational reasoning goes away. Not because it has to go away, but because we have trained our bodies for it to go away. We have created muscle memory that signals us to let loose with our words when we reach a certain frustration point.

Suddenly…

It's okay to call names.

It's okay to swear.

It's okay to attack the person's character.

It's okay to say things we "don't really mean."

Except that it is *not* okay to do any of these things. Even in the midst of our anger, we need to control these things. That's why the guy who "has to yell at his wife or kids" can refrain from yelling at his boss because he (wrongly) believes that the consequences of yelling at his boss, namely the loss of his job, will be worse than the consequences of his abusive behavior toward his loved ones.

Exploders are not the only ones who act like they are slaves to their emotions. Hunters, as I call them, are the most obvious ones who simply react. They're also people who shut down (rabbits). Eventually, they may explode, emotionally sit out, or both; but initially, they withdraw.

They punish by not talking. They ignore.

When I meet with them, they want me to believe that they cannot help it. But I cannot believe that.

I refuse to believe that.

Rather, I affirm that they can help themselves. They can choose to interact in a way that isn't destructive. They can simply state what happened and how they felt about it without attacking the person. They do not have to yell. They do not have to swear or call names.

They can engage other people in a way that builds the relationship, not destroy it.

This is a skill that can be learned and quite frankly *has* to be learned. We can control our impulses. The question is always how?

First, we need to have a plan. Think through your last two or three major disagreements with your partner or spouse. My guess is that they probably followed a pattern from beginning to end. In fact, my guess is that for many of you, there came a point in the conversation or argument when you made an intentional decision to set the fire. You purposely set it off because you were upset, scared, hurt, or frustrated—or all of the above. You reacted out of muscle memory.

A response is what is needed in almost every fight that couples have. By using a response, they can mitigate the tension that is inherent in every conflict in their lives.

This involves foresight. Write down your most common response when you are fighting that is destructive. Can you identify the thought process that leads you to that statement? If so, write it down as well.

Now we plan.

Write down what you will say the next time you have that thought process. Focus on what you will do, not only what you *won't* do. If you are normally a name caller, you might write down, "I will focus on behaviors in my next conflict. I will not call names." If you know the specific behavior that will probably irritate you, you can write that down as well. You might want to consider role-playing through the conflict.

I know it will feel a little weird at first—standing in your living room or bedroom practicing a fight—but feeling weird is a small price to pay to develop your skills as navigating the circle of conflict.

BADFIT is simply a guide map for how to better handle your conflict. The three core questions let you know what the target is that you are shooting for in all conflict. If you can make the target of answering those three questions in the affirmative for your loved one, traversing conflict will be a positive for your relationship.

Ultimately, it is up to you what you say and do in a conflict situation in your relationship. You can choose to talk about anything without adding fuel to the fire. It is difficult. It is hard. It is doable.

There is a cheat code that can help you achieve this in your relationship. It is difficult. It is hard. It is doable.

You can give your partner permission to call you out when you violate one of the six rules. In other words, if you are attacking her, instead of talking about what she did, you should give her permission to point out that you are attacking the person, not the issue.

If you are jumping from one point to the next without actually giving time for a solution to the first problem, you should give your husband permission to point out that you are not staying on track with today's news. This "calling out" will be so frustrating at first, but it offers you real-time accountability.

Yes, you will probably become angrier—at first. Yes, you will want to scream or run away depending on your natural bend, but eventually those responses will go away and you will become a conflict ninja. Being intentional is the lynchpin that holds everything else together when you are working on building your relationship.

Without intentionality, all the best planning in the world will not help you respond correctly.

A Word about Failing

As you try to change your interactions through conflict, you will fail. I guarantee it. Change is hard. It takes time. You have to come back to it over and over again.

An often overlooked aspect to being intentional is getting back up off the floor and trying again. Being intentional might mean that you ask for forgiveness. It might mean that you forgive your partner—*again*.

Being intentional means that you put your relationship above everything else, including how you feel in the moment.

2. Always Avoid Always and Never Say Never

A common but destructive tactic couples employ is the utilization of universal statements about what the other person does. This often leads to the couple arguing over the validity of the universal claim. An example might look like the following conversation I overheard once:

Woman: You always ignore me when I want to talk about politics.

Man: No, I don't. I haven't done it for at least three days. Just the other day, I listened to you rant on and on about how bad (fill in politician's name) is and how we're all doomed.

Female: See! You're always so judgmental!

Male: You never want to talk about anything else.

Female: Because if I don't want to talk about your

precious football or damn music, I don't want to talk about anything important.

Notice how the conversation devolved because each person was arguing against the universal statements, not the actual problem. That's the problem with universal statements: they automatically increase the defensiveness of our partner. It hides the real hurt and problem behind statements that sound as though they are designed to tear down rather than build up.

Think about human nature for a moment. Most of us will think of the exception to what's being said even if we don't voice that exception. When the words are leveled at us, we tend to double down on this natural instinct. This works against emotional security and fosters distrust.

I almost always add the word *almost* when I hear someone say "always" or "never" in my head. I cannot think of a time when I have seen those types of universal words used in a manner that benefited the conversation or the relationship attached to that conversation. Those words are used to end the conversation. It's the adult equivalent of, "I'm right, you're wrong, nah nah nah!" To have an emotionally secure relationship, you need to use words that invite conversation with your spouse.

Even if you do not want to invite conversation, using these words will often derail you from your actual goal. Look at the example above. Do you see something that moves toward her real problem? The real reason she wanted to talk in the first place? I see an interaction devolving into a shouting match, where emotions are escalating and dialogue is dying.

When your partner uses a universal statement, you have a choice. You can seize on that problem or you can invite dialogue. You might ask, "Could you tell me more?" By utilizing this technique, you are showing interest in building the relationship.[2]

This avoids a final problem with these types of statements: they show only self-interest. There is little interest in understanding the other person's point of view on the topic. It moves the conversation and the couple away from shared understanding and toward misunderstanding and hurt. Healthy couples seek to understand each other's point of view before they respond.

When I teach this principle in marriage conferences, I often use the following example:

Wife: You never do this!

Husband: That's not true. I think it was six years ago. Fall. It had just rained…

That silly illustration shows the absurdity of our conversations when we engage in unhealthy strategies.

3. Does It Have to Be a Problem?

So much of what happens doesn't have to be a problem. The difference between couples who are doing well and couples who are on the verge of divorce is the fact that the couple who is in a good place knows that not everything has to be a problem. For couples

---

2 To see a longer, more in-depth conversation visit www.emotionallysecurecouple.com.

who are in trouble, everything is a problem. They have very little ability to tolerate stress of disagreement for bad situations.

In my experience and based on my reading of various studies, couples across the health spectrum have the same degree of what I call *flash points*. Flash points are those times that could devolve into a fight if one or either person pushes the emotional status just a little more toward the fight, or they can pull back just a little.

It is their belief regarding the necessity of something being a problem that will often make the difference. If a person believes that every slight, every difference, must be addressed, they will often be willing to push into the fight. Sometimes, perhaps often, the best thing that can be done is to just let it go. Whatever it is.

But what does need to be a problem and what doesn't? The answer is going to look differently for each couple and I like to teach what I call the 5-5-5 rule.

The rule basically states this: If in 5 hours, 5 weeks, or 5 years, you are standing at your spouse's grave, will whatever you are stressed about currently be a problem? If the answer is that it will not be a problem at the graveside, then it probably doesn't have to be a problem now. I am often told this sounds both radical and unreasonable, but is it?

Is it truly unreasonable to choose to err on the side of believing in your spouse and your relationship? How many fights have you gone through and then later, you couldn't remember what started it? How many times have you decided later that you were just tired or hungry? I strongly believe that most of the fights couples have are harmful because they are unnecessary in the first place.

I often tell couples that they just need twenty minutes of serious self-control. Twenty minutes of just walking away or acting as though nothing is bothering them and the urge to fight will continually pass. The twenty minutes has a second benefit. It allows the fire to burn down, often helping us to avoid a fight over something that doesn't really need to be a problem and it helps us have a better perspective for the things that do have to be a problem.

When a couple can take twenty minutes to begin processing their distress, they may decide that "it" *does* have to be a problem. When this happens and they have developed the habit of slowing things down by waiting for an intentional time period, they can begin to formulate how they will approach the conflict with their spouse. This intentionality gives the conversation the benefit of being engineered to express the problem without unnecessarily increasing the defensiveness.

Let's move on to the final three rules of BADFIT.

Chapter 18:

The Six Rules

(#4–6 of BADFIT)

4. Facts Only

WHEN YOU ENGAGE IN CONFLICT, IT IS IMPERATIVE to deal in facts only. Dealing with only the facts is one of the hardest skills you can develop as a human being. It's not that I think most people are liars; I think that most people assume they are right even about what they are assuming.

This is a really important distinction. Think about how many times you and your partner have had a fight when things went really wrong, really quickly. Usually, something is said and your partner reacts to what you think you understand the person to be saying. You take what they say and run out seven or eight evolutions in your brain—making interpretations and assumptions the entire way. Often, the response is based on the conclusions of those evolutions, not on what they actually said and rarely on what they meant.

This is the difference in discussing or arguing over what we know versus what we *think* we know. Often, we respond to what we *think* we know.

Erica: I'm frustrated that the trash didn't get out today.

Joe: (Thinking she's frustrated at him) Well, I had to get to work early today. Why didn't you do it? I can't do everything around the house, you know...

Do you see the inherent problem with how Joe reacted? He immediately assumed that Erica was frustrated with him. The truth is that she might be upset and frustrated with him, but he doesn't know that. He's dealing with an assumption, not a fact. Because he's arguing from his assumption, he's becoming more defensive, which will almost always prompt him to use words that cause his spouse's defensive levels to increase. It is relatively easy to see how this fight could move all over the place and both parties feel like they were simultaneously right and yet, have no real idea what they were fighting over.

Let's look at another way Joe could have handled this conversation:

Erica: I'm frustrated that the trash didn't get out today.

Joe: You're frustrated because we have trash piling up? That sucks.

Erica: Yes, this whole new day just messes my schedule up.

Joe: Are you frustrated with me, or just because the trash didn't get out? (Joe asks this because in their family, Erica has always been the one who takes out the trash, and yet, Joe was tempted to assume that Erica was frustrated with him.)

Erica: No, I'm just upset because I have no idea how we're going to get all of this trash out of here.

Joe: Yeah, that stinks… uh no pun intended…

In the second conversation, Joe uses the Mirror Method to make sure he understands what is Erica's true source of frustration. He doesn't react, rather he responds in a way that allows him a means to diffuse his own defensiveness as well as actively working to show empathy to Erica regarding her frustration.

I get the sense that many times when someone is frustrated, it has little or nothing to do with their partner. However, the frustration works like a prime of explosives. When your spouse senses that you are upset, they begin to feel the tension of that frustration and they react. They begin to defend themselves and then something sets off the spark and the fight begins.

Dealing with only the facts allows us a method to make sure we are responding to what is actually happening without being enslaved to react to what we think is going on. It gives us the means to be proactive in our arguments without being caught up in reactions to things that might not even be a problem. Of course, it is easy to illustrate what happens when our assumption is wrong, but what about when it's right? What do we do when we think we know what our spouse is really upset about, but we're uncertain?

Simply put: we do the same thing. We don't assume we know until we actually hear them say it. We can only deal with facts as we know them. If your partner hasn't said something, then you don't have facts to deal with at this point.

Let's pretend that Erica was upset with Joe because she thought he was going to take out the trash. What might that conversation look like in regards to our "facts only" component?

Erica: I'm frustrated the trash didn't get out today.

Joe: You're frustrated because we missed the trash and now it's going to pile up?

Erica: Yes.

Joe: Are you frustrated with me?

Erica: Yes, I thought you were going to take it out before you left for work.

Joe now has facts to respond to in a way that helps solve the problem. Maybe he has a good reason the trash didn't get out, maybe he doesn't, but he has done the work necessary to respond to the facts. He doesn't have to be defensive, nor does he have to get to the end of the argument and wonder what the whole thing was about. He might say something like the following:

Joe: Well, I'm a little confused by that. Did you tell me you were expecting me to take out the trash and I didn't hear you? You normally are the one who takes out the trash so I just assumed you would continue doing it. Should I adjust that assumption?

Notice here that Joe isn't blaming. He's expressing his confusion and the assumptions that he was operating out of. He's further asking Erica if he should adjust those assumptions and alter his actions. This is the bones of a great conversation, even though there is frustration and confusion in it. He may have been feeling somewhat defensive, but he was able to hold two divergent feelings in tension: feeling defensive and feeling confused. His confusion probably created some of the defensiveness he was feeling, so his response was to seek clarification.

This is also an excellent response when we are being told about something wrong with us. I think it is especially true that we tend to get defensive when we are being told we did something wrong or there is something we need to change. The more defensive we are, the more likely we are to react and go on the offensive in one way or another. By using the Mirror Method to ferret out the actual facts of the situation, we are more likely to solve the conflict rather than set fire to the other person's emotions.

WHAT HAPPENS IF WE DISAGREE ON THE FACTS?

You've followed the steps, and you both still disagree on the facts. This is probably most common when we find ourselves in the classic "he said, she said" disagreement.

When this happens, first accept that there is a disagreement. Problems often develop when I ask couples to define the nature of the disagreement. In part, this is because in our modern parlance, we use words we don't actually mean. We say, "What you said was…" when we really mean, "How I interpreted what you said was…" This is so common and so destructive.

Kristy and Jeremy came to see me for a variety of issues. There had been infidelity and enough hurt to pass around a few times over. They had four children, all girls, and they were trying to piece their marriage back together. Their worldviews had drastically changed over the years and their belief about how to engage conflict had devolved. Of course, I was asking them to pull those scabs off and go after the potential pain and payoff of engaging the conflict. They recently had a severe disagreement that had actually begun two weeks before our session. On their way to our session, the smoldering fire had resurfaced so that they had walked into our time together rather heated.

I asked them what was going on, and words poured out in a torrent of verbal vomit as they both scrambled to explain their side of the story. After a few moments of clarifying questions, I asked them to begin discussing it with each other. I almost always make each person wait to respond until after the first person is done talking for at least the first evolution of the conversation. For clarity, I refer to one person making a statement and the partner or spouse responding as one evolution.

After the first evolution, I may just let the conversation run for a few moments if I believe it is therapeutically beneficial as I did in this case.

During their conversation, it became clear that they were arguing over what Kristy felt she said versus what Jeremy thought she said. He repeatedly said, "Well, that's what I heard!"

As I'm sure you know, that conversation will burn a long time and rarely get anywhere. At some point, they must agree to disagree. The conversation does not have to end there. They could both ask how they might do better at clarifying the next time something similar comes up.[3]

FIND CLARIFICATION

Many times, the disagreement is over the meaning of the words used, not the words. We think the words they used mean something different than what they thought they meant. When we strive to deal with facts only, we work to ensure that we are only responding to what the person is actually saying, not what we think they may be saying. If our interpretation of what they are saying is not an easily made and literal interpretation, then we should utilize the Mirror Method to make sure our interpretation is accurate.

In the situation of Jeremy and Kristy, Jeremy was already dialed up because he was feeling the pressure

---

3   For a deeper look at this conversation visit,
     www.emotionallysecurecouple.com.

of believing he had failed because of a past situation. He knew that this was a stress point for his wife in the past and they had talked about it. He had come up with ways he could do it better, and that night those better methods had simply not been implemented. He was already primed to be defensive and when his wife showed obvious signs of frustration, he immediately defended by attacking. In fact, at one point in our session, she asked him why he was yelling and he said, "Because I'm mad!" As he sorted out what he knew versus what he *thought* he knew, Jeremy realized he was actually more frustrated with himself and the kids. His anger with his wife was minimal.

WHAT DO YOU DO WHEN YOUR SPOUSE IS MAD AT YOU?

This brings us to the third way to deal with the facts only: what do you do when you know your spouse is mad at you?

By now, I imagine you're getting the idea that we do the same thing as the other two scenarios. If you know your spouse or partner is angry with you, it is important to still deal with the facts. When we know we are wrong, we are most tempted to be defensive and more importantly, we are most tempted to "be right."

When I'm talking about this principle in a session, I often tell clients that I am not calling anyone a liar; I'm simply saying that as humans, we are never more tempted to stretch the truth to "be right." This obviously puts the relationship foundation of love, trust, and respect in danger. It is important to deal with only facts no matter how the conversation is going because that allows us to stay on topic (an important principle dealt with in the rule called "Today's News"). When we use this method to stay on track, we will be less likely to have aimless arguments that only seem to hurt our partner and damage our relationship.

5. Issues Only

Dealing with only the issues means we deal with the problems, not the person. This seems like such a no-brainer, but think about all the times you've had an argument go south when the person has been attacked, or when you have felt attacked. Too often, our words move from dealing with the person's actions and attack the person. Then, after the fight is over, even though we know we were wrong, we also know we were right. Apologizing becomes a painful act because the whole situation becomes a bloody and muddy mess of hurt and miscommunication.

To deal with the issues only, you have to commit to thinking through what you say before you say it. I know this sounds so simple, but experience should tell you just how hard it is. Most people have bad habits in the way that they communicate, which causes them to increase the stress in a conversation and the relationship.

No one wants to be defined by their mistakes. No

one wants to be defined by their failures.

Yet, that is how most people attempt to paint their partner when they are in an argument with them. They use "you are" words instead of "you did" words. This moves the problem from something that can be fixed to something that your partner *is*.

It dials up the problem into something loud and insurmountable. It tells your spouse that you believe they have a fundamental flaw in them that can't be changed without fundamentally altering who they are. It increases their defensiveness. We must constantly consider how our words are affecting our partner's defensiveness. Are the words used causing the defensiveness to increase or decrease? Everyone involved will already be somewhat defensive, as they will be stressed.

But the attack of their person increases that defensiveness and stress exponentially. It pushes both parties toward the fight or flight mode.

Dealing with issues also helps to keep the discussion on point. We're not tempted to wander with our discussion when we are only dealing with issues. We decrease the chances that our spouse is going to respond with something random as a defense mechanism. Because of that, we create a space where a conversation regarding the real possibility of change is discussed.

Dealing with the issues keeps us from causing pain that we will regret later and still gives us a clear path to express our own frustration and feelings. It allows us to have a beginning, middle, and end to the argument or discussion. Everyone has disagreements. Everyone has feelings of frustration and sometimes even real anger, and everyone can choose not to attack their partner in those moments.

That's really what I'm talking about in this section: you do not have to attack your partner. You do not have to say hurtful things. That is always a choice. Hurting someone with your words will often feel good in the moment, but over the long run, they actually cause damage to the things you value the most: relationships.

Sometimes, your spouse will feel hurt or attacked because they are hearing things they do not want to hear about what they have done. How they decide to handle that is on them. At other times, they will have a legitimate complaint about being attacked. Changing that is on us.

The key is to have agreed-upon ground rules for how discussions should happen. What words are acceptable and which words are not to be used should be decided before the disagreement actually happens. One of those agreed-upon ground rules should be that only words that deal with actions will be used and words that deal with a person's being will not be used.

This means that we commit to using action verbs. We talk about what the partner/spouse did or did not do, not who they are. This inherently allows them the possibility of change.

So often, our legitimate complaints become bogged down because we attack the person. No one wants to be defined by their mistakes.

EMMA AND JOSH

Emma and Josh had been married for three years when they came to see me. They had two children who were both young. Emma worked part time at her family business and felt worn out most of the time. Josh was moving ahead quickly in his company. From the outside, they had the perfect marriage. But tears fell freely as Emma explained to me that they "simply could not communicate!" Josh agreed and they were at their wit's end.

I asked them what they thought was keeping them from communicating. They both responded with, "I don't know." I have found this to be a rather common answer to this question so I usually ask a few follow-up questions in reserve to attempt to push the conversation forward.

Emma: He's just so angry all of the time!

Me: What do you mean?

Emma: He just yells at me nonstop.

Josh: Well, that's not entirely true. She's always so grumpy with me. It's like—

Emma: Oh, sure, it's all *my* fault. (Notice they are quickly devolving into the mutual blame conversation).

Emma: He's just a yeller.

Josh: And she's just a complainer! She's never happy!

Emma: What about you? You just come home and sit down like I'm you're servant and you're some king! It's like you think because you work, I don't need your help at home. I almost feel like you're just lazy.

Josh: There you go! She's also just mean when she gets mad. Out in public, she'll be all nice and then bam! We get home and she's as mean as a hornet.

Some readers will think this conversation may have gone too far down too fast to be real, but I suspect that many readers will recognize it as not only plausible but as part of their story. Emma started off okay. She stated that he's angry a lot. This could be improved a little bit, but for the most part, it's a decent way to engage into the circle of conflict.

Trouble came when Josh began to disagree with her. She could have improved her statements by talking about what exactly Josh did and only what he did. Josh also fell apart because he started talking about her and not her actions.[4]

By dealing with the actions, which is the real problem, we offer love and hope to our spouse. We demonstrate that we can love them, but at the same time need to find a way for them to change a few things while we ourselves find a way to change.

Relationships are about loving each other where you are and at the same time, pushing each other to

4   To see how the conversation could have gone differently visit, www.emotioanallysccurecouple.com.

be better. Most people are willing to take the pushing if they believe that they are being pushed because the other person loves them.

A Note about Words and Actions

Words are actions when it comes to relationships. While we are conditioned in our society that the two are different, they are not when it comes to relationships. At least one entire book could be filled discussing the differences and similarities of actions and words.

When you are discussing someone's words, say you understood what was said and how you interpreted it. With the ubiquitousness of text messaging, so many couples have entire discussions over text. Often, the words can be read to mean multiple things.

Tone often has more to do with how we read it than how the person typed it. This combination can lead to disaster when it comes to discussions and relationships.

This also leads to a second problem spot: when the couple actually argues over what was said. When this happens, it is really important to use the Mirror Method to come to a consensus on what was said. This can be helpful when what you heard is not what your partner meant to say.

Of course, if there is always a debate about what was said versus what was heard, that may be an issue in and of itself that needs to be discussed.

6. Today's News

One of the biggest derailments for fights is their lack of direction. A disagreement starts out dealing with one issue, and then it begins to experience conversational drift. As the conversation drifts, it often becomes heated from burning emotions. It can begin to move at a frenetic pace that is not only illogical but destructive to the emotional security of the relationship.

Staying on track is done by only dealing with the issue at hand. I call this today's news.

Dealing with today's news is about facing the issue or issues in front of you and refusing to move in any other direction. It's about staying engaged in a manner that allows you to solve the problem without bringing up past hurts.

When you do this, you can engage the problem and refuse to leave it; you can communicate to your partner that you care about them. You tell your spouse that you want what is best for the relationship and for them.

By engaging today's news, you can offer hope to your spouse that you are actually interested in finding a way to solve the problem. It tells them that you care about them enough to share a problem and that you are in love enough to want to solve that problem instead of just attacking them.

Today's news allows the past to be the past. It doesn't avoid the conflict, but it refuses to bring up every sin from the past to be used as a weapon. When couples follow this rule, they force themselves to deal with the issue at hand until it is solved. By doing this, they minimize the amount of intentional hurt that they might inflict on their partner if they allow the conversation to run across the emotional landscape. By staying on track, the couple increases their chances of solving the problem and coming to the place where they can put the issue to rest.

This is the second strong advantage of this rule. By sticking with today's news, we can't ignore something simply because engaging it will make us uncomfortable. When we do this (avoid), we essentially ingest poison. Slow-acting but often fatal poison that destroys us, our relationships, and almost anything that touches our soul.

Today's news forces us to deal with issues as they arise. It doesn't allow for us to ignore an issue because we feel uncomfortable. While we do not have to deal with something immediately, we do have to deal with it relatively soon. This allows us to process it and move on rather than allowing the anger to fester and rot.

Eric's eyes lit up when I brought up this topic at a Hopes and Dreams Marriage Conference I was teaching a few years ago. Hopes and Dreams Marriage Conferences are something my wife and I have been doing for almost a decade now, teaching these principles to as many people as possible. Eric's entire body twitched when I began talking about this rule.

At the break, he came up to me rather excited and told me that his wife was constantly bringing up everything that happened over the course of their marriage. Worse, in his eyes, she was incredibly passive-aggressive in how she talked about the past. "It's like she has a movie-like memory for things that happened fifteen years ago!" he exclaimed.

Later, the three of us were meeting and it went something like the following:

Eric: Well, like I told you at the conference, Mandy seems to remember everything I've ever done wrong. I hear about them every time I do something new that's wrong.

Mandy: (interrupting) That's not exactly true—he's just an exaggerator.

Eric: See, I'm wrong again.

Mandy: Well, you are! This is just like the other day when you told me how I never praise you for doing anything right around the house. You always just want praise.

Eric: Okay, here's an example: the other day, we were talking about vacation this summer. I came home from work and sat down in my chair to just relax for a few moments. I had a long day. She came home and was upset because I hadn't moved some stuff in the garage. Somehow, that spun to this time eight years ago when I blew up on vacation. What do the two have to do with each other?

Mandy: A lot. They illustrate exactly how selfish you can be.

At this point, I interrupted and asked Mandy for clarification of what she meant by selfish. She swallowed hard, sat forward on the couch, and told me she was glad I asked.

Mandy: When we were dating, he went out with his friends and got drunk. He ended up flirting with some slut!

Almost immediately, Eric jumped in and pointed out that they had been married for over fifteen years so this was at least seventeen years ago.

And while he was 100 percent correct that this offense had been seventeen years ago, it had never been dealt with so it became a magnet for every pain, insult, and injury to follow. When we fail to deal with today's news, it becomes yesterday's news—but worse, it becomes unprocessed news.

This leads to a wound that never heals. Unhealed wounds become infected and cause more pain. Eventually, they cause death.

When we deal with the issues today, we stop infections from starting. Furthermore, we tell our partner that we love them and care about the relationship enough to engage in something that they inherently fear. This creates ground for emotional security to grow.

Chapter 19:

Building Emotional Security beyond Words

ONE OF THE BIGGEST MISTAKES I SEE PEOPLE engage in over and over again is that they don't allow their partner to have a win. They push for change in some way and their partner works on that change. Then the rules change.

This would be like playing baseball and hitting a home run only to have the umpire not allow the run because he decided the rules would be different for you. Imagine that frustration. Imagine the anger that would present in that situation.

So many relationships that are full of anger have this problem running through them in excess.

Ask yourself if you give your spouse a way to win. When you ask them to do something and they do it, do you say thank you without adding any additional criteria or criticism? If they do something that you don't like, do you explain to them how it could be done in the manner you would like? One of my favorite questions to ask in therapy is, "What does it (whatever it is) look like when it's done right?"

Do you give clear expectations of what you want and need? Take a moment to write out what you want in your relationship.

Take a look at your list. Go through and draw a line through all of the items that are actually things you *don't* want. A true problem in many relationships is that we don't know what we want; we simply know what we *don't* want. Imagine asking your partner what he or she wanted for dinner. They reply that they don't want pizza. Does that actually help? Not much. It tells you what they don't want, but it fails to mention what they *do* want. When you can't articulate what you want, your partner doesn't know what they are aiming to hit. They don't know the target.

This creates frustration and pain. As humans, we avoid pain. It's hardwired into most of us. This hard wiring keeps us safe. It helps us live long and somewhat prosperous lives. But what happens when a person you want to spend that long and prosperous life with is the source of your pain? You avoid them. You morph the pain from the activity to them. You associate it with them.

I once heard a story about a woman who had been raped on a school bus. She had been out for a walk and was attacked, dragged into a bus, and assaulted. For many years after, she would have a panic attack whenever she would see a yellow school bus. If one drove by her house, she would begin to sweat and struggle to breathe. Why?

The bus posed no real threat to her. But she associated it with the most painful moment in her life. Seeing the bus triggered an avalanche of painful and hurtful memories for her. Her body associated the pain of her assault with the yellow bus. Sadly, I have seen this same thing happen with couples. One person, sometimes both, begins to associate their partner with the pain of the relationship. In their mind, the problem isn't the pain—it's actually their partner. So what do we do? How do we articulate what we want from our spouse? We need to aim for three guideposts. We need to make sure that what we want is 100 percent in their control, measurable, and clear.

THREE GUIDEPOSTS OF GOOD COMMUNICATION

1. 100 percent in their control

When I ask people what they want from their spouse, I often hear unhelpful things like, "I want him to make me happy" or "I want her to do better at making me feel loved." These are not helpful statements. They are extremely damaging and negative statements. We can't help someone else feel happy. We can do things that foster that happiness, but ultimately they must choose to be happy. We can't make someone feel loved, but we can cultivate ground through actions that helps them feel loved.

Whatever you ask of your spouse must be 100 percent in their control. So if Sally's husband carving out time every Friday for her is one of the ways she feels loved, she needs to articulate that to him. He doesn't have to agree to meet that need, but at least it is completely in his control. He can choose to meet her need or choose not to meet it. He can want to meet it but believe that it is outside of his available resources. The choice is completely his to make. This is empowering.

2. Measurable

Imagine that you are having a conversation with your spouse and he tells you he wants to be a bigger priority in your life. How do you feel? What does that mean? How much is a bigger priority? If you made yourself completely available to do something with him two times last year, and you double that this year, would that meet his criteria? I mean, technically, he moved up the priority list. Yet, somehow, I doubt he would feel like his desire was met. Why? Because it wasn't measurable.

Now, let's pretend that your partner said she wanted to go on at least two dates just the two of you every month for the next year. That is a measurable statement. It allows you to look back over the year and measure whether or not you went out two dates a month. Words only have meaning because we give them meaning. The color blue is only blue because we've decided as a society to call it blue. Our relationships get into trouble when we start using words that have more nebulous meanings. Words like *more, better,* or *higher* aren't helpful because, while they are technically measurable, they are not clear on what the measurable goal is.

Think about someone who wants to lose some weight or get healthier. This person's chance of sticking to a workout and better eating routine is slim because the goal is not really measurable. Now, if they change it to, "I want to lose ten pounds by August 1," or "I want to not eat junk food more than once a week for the next three months," they are setting measurable goals for themselves. Four couples, this might look like, "I want us to go away once a quarter, just the two of us." Maybe someone feels security from having a certain number in the savings account. They need to articulate that amount to their spouse rather than simply stating that they want to feel more secure in the relationship. By stating what they want in a measurable manner, they create the opportunity for continued conversation and evaluation about how the relationship is progressing. This also allows their partner to feel empowered in the relationship. Activities become about us working together toward a goal that we can actually see.

Maybe Sally wants Steve to turn off the television when she is talking to him, but she just says to him, "I want you to focus on me when I'm talking to you, not watch TV." So the next night, she begins talking to him and he turns the volume way down on his favorite show but still keeps one eye on the screen.

Sally becomes incensed because she can't believe that just twenty-four hours after talking to him about this, he's not making her a priority. Steve senses her anger but is confused because in his mind, he is making her a priority. He doesn't know that she is measuring this conversation by the TV being off or on. This is often a great catalyst for a big fight because now Steve is going to be defensive and have his own feelings hurt.

This brings up another important reason that making our needs measurable is important, because we all have some measuring stick in our brain to determine the success or failure of our spouse's attempt to meet our needs. It's important that we share that measurement with our spouse. This helps them to better understand what they are aiming for and how they can best meet our needs and move the relationship forward. We are always either building the relationship up or tearing it down—there is no in-between, no middle ground.

3. Clear

This one can be a little confusing for people I walk with on the journey toward emotional security. It seems too simple. I have even had interns tell me that this one seems like such a no-brainer, until they sit in a room with a couple and hear their unclear expectations.

We don't do it intentionally, but as humans, we simply seem to have a hard time articulating what we want. Ask someone what she wants to feel loved and she will tell you what she doesn't want to happen. Ask someone what his spouse can do so that he can feel like a priority and he will tell you about what the spouse shouldn't do, often in a rambling and rather incoherent stream of consciousness.

It's not that it's not okay to say what we don't want. You should be able to articulate to your spouse what you don't want in the relationship and your partner should respect those wishes.

But life is about more than *not doing*. Life is built through doing. Relationships are put together through doing and giving. Doing for the other person is the giving of ourselves. By stating clearly what we would like to see happen, we give our spouse the opportunity to better understand us.

We attempt to connect actions to emotions through this process. One person states what they want to happen and what that looks like to them. The other person then has the opportunity to say yes, no, or offer a compromise. This is part of the way that two people become bonded. They work through disagreements about what should happen.

Sometimes, one person does something simply because the other person wants to do it. Sometimes, they refuse. Other times, they offer a compromise and sometimes both parties just agree to sit in the tension of disagreeing. These steps are the building blocks of the beautiful dance that constitutes relationships.

By being clear about what we are hoping to see happen, we ensure that our partner knows what a win is for the situation. I believe that most people want their partner to be happy and they want to do what they can (or believe that they can) do to help facilitate that happiness. Often, the problem is truly that they don't know what that looks like for their spouse.

This confusion can lead to trouble because we tend to fill in the blanks on our own. Sometimes, a person will put a lot of time into something that they think will be good for the relationship, only to find out that their spouse hates it. This doubles the pain. Clarity allows us to minimize the possibility that we will confuse our partner.

A temptation can be to move from one problem to another without solving the first issue. The danger in this is that it robs your spouse of the opportunity to feel as though they are winning and therefore your relationship is winning. Winning means your relationship is improving. When there is no clear win, you could sow discouragement and hurt the health of your relationship over time.

Chapter 20:

Conclusion

I HOPE THIS BOOK WAS A GOOD STARTING PLACE FOR you in your relationship. It is not the final word on relationships, but my hope is that it will bring healing to those who need it. My desire is that every couple finds a way to be healthy. I believe that every relationship can be healthy and a safe place when both people want the relationship to work and when they are both ready to change.

The principles in this book need to be practiced. If you want to get better at anything, you need to practice it. If you'd like more information about how to do that or would like to watch videos of people practicing these skills, connect with me at www.joemartino.com.

If your relationship is in trouble, please give counseling a try. If you have tried in the past and it didn't work, try a different therapist. Successful therapy is predicated off of a good relationship between the couple and the therapist. Not every therapist works well for every couple. I have been successful where other therapists have not, and other therapists have been successful where I have failed.

Most importantly, please know that I believe any couple can come back from anything if they both want the relationship to work and they are both willing to change. I believe in you.

Acknowledgments

THE IDEA OF TRYING TO RECOGNIZE EVERYONE WHO has helped me bring this book to fruition is a daunting and scary task. I am sure I will miss someone.

Thank you to my family for all the time giving up to my figuring this book out. Thanks to Tom for always believing in me and putting action behind that belief.

Thank you to everyone who read early versions and offered constructive feedback. Thank you to Shayla for editing, and Kara for designing the cover.

Thank you to all the couples who have allowed me to walk with them through the often painful journey of marriage and relationship counseling.

About the Author

JOE MARTINO IS A LICENSED THERAPIST IN MICHIGAN and the author of *The Emotionally Secure Couple*. He specializes in relationship therapy. His goal is to change the world by helping one couple at a time have the healthiest relationship possible. He is passionate in his belief that everyone can have the relationship they dreamed of having.

He and his wife cofounded the Joe Martino Counseling Network. They have been married for 19 years and have four children. They live on a small hobby farm with their three dogs and two cats.

Joe has an eclectic collection of hobbies, enjoying the outdoors and spending time in museums or bookstores. Connect with him on his website at www.joemartino.com or on twitter @joemartino.

When it comes to marriages, too many people ask the wrong question. They ask, "Will we make it?"

Relationship therapist Joe Martino wants people to ask, "Will we be glad we made it?" He believes that every couple can make it and be excited that they did.

In this book, you'll learn:

- A cogent definition for what communication is and how you can be better at it.
- Four dangerous ways couples interact in their relationship.
- Why conflict is your best friend.
- A proven way to have more productive conversations even when you're mad at your partner.
- How to discuss anything in a way that builds the relationship.
- Three core questions that you both are asking and how to answer them.

Each chapter is written in an easy-to-understand manner and comes with discussion questions to help further your understanding of the material. *The Emotionally Secure Couple* can be read alone or with your partner for a deeper experience as a couple.

If you really want to take your experience to the next level, grab a couple of friends and read the book as a group discussion.

For more information, study guides, and videos by the author exclusively for readers, go to www.emotionallysecurecouple.com.

Made in the USA
San Bernardino, CA
02 March 2018